One Thing for Certain,

Two Things for Sure

Craig Stewart

Published by Craig Stewart

Impeccable Works, LLC

www.CraigTheWriterStewart.com

Cover Photography and Design by: Justin J. Jordan

ArtistDirector Media

www.ArtistDirector.info

Back cover photo by KuFunya Kail Photography

ISBN-13:978-0692442043
ISBN-10:0692442049

Legal Disclaimer

This book is based, in part, upon actual events, persons, and companies. However, numerous characters, incidents and companies portrayed and the names used herein are fictitious. Any similarity of those fictitious characters, incidents, or companies to the name attributes or actual background of any actual person, living or dead, or to any actual event, or to any existing company, is entirely coincidental, and unintentional.

While the author has made every effort to provide accurate telephone numbers and Internet addresses at the time of publication, neither the publisher nor the author assumes any responsibility for errors, or for changes that occur after publication. Further, the publisher does not have any control over and does not assume any responsibility for author or third-party websites of their content.

Also by Craig Stewart:

Words Never Spoken, A Memoir

CONTENTS

ACKNOWLEDGMENTS

To the women in my life,

Behind every success is a story filled with setbacks, days of hopelessness and thoughts of giving up. Most times we never hear that part of the dream because most people are only interested in the dream realized.

Behind my story is a line of women who picked me up, dusted me off, fed me, bandaged my wounds, or simply told me along the journey, "***Don't give up, you're too close***" when I wanted to quit. In that line stands many women known by just a few—until now. First in that line is my mother, Gladys Stewart. Thank you for consistency. I can always trust your instincts when I'm unsure if I can trust my own.

Angela Marie Bolin, Danielle M. Brown, Sherri Brown, Kelli Purcell Wright, Shannon Morgan, Gena Pemberton, Kim Davis, Tara Williams, Kina Cosper, Georgiana Threats, Juanita Jones, Mariam Lynn Sydnor, Leah E. Williams, my sister JaDonna Allen, my aunt Gloria Chambers, and my cousin Tiffany Goodman.

Special Thanks...

Mr. Elliott Bryan Williams, thank you for nudging me to write this follow up to *Words Never Spoken*, and for sharing your space with me to create. Freddie Mae lives on in you.

Rashard Smith, Felecia Townser, Mikael Thompson, Kevin O. Fogle, Lisa Gausney, Kimberly-Howell Johnson, Cameron Hartwill, Marion Jamell Lessington, Will Brown, Patricia Spaulding, Toni Nelson, Tanika Humphrey-Cabral, Brandon Thompson, Dr. Thomas McBryde, Scott Bogan, Terry Hooks, Wendell Carter, Richard Moultrie, John Gripper, Juan Gaddis, Isoul Harris, Dr. Neal Foster, The Stuarts and Tim Daniels for your willingness to always lend a hand to help push my dream forward.

Thank you for breathing *life* into my dreams...

LEAVING ATLANTA

**The following is the last chapter of Craig Stewart's first novel,
Words Never Spoken, A Memoir. It's recommended that you
read it also—*One Thing for Certain, Two Things for Sure* is
the sequel.**

Friendships weren't the only things being recycled in
Atlanta. There was a line of gay men at a revolving door waiting
their turn to date the same men, but the trend didn't stop there.
The same was true of the gyms, nightclubs, and apartment
complexes that we flocked to as they sprouted up in the city. We
were in search of something or someone. It was like watching a
merry go round of people taking turns sleeping with the same
people. The usual six degrees of separation was more like two
degrees in Atlanta—part of the reason HIV is running rampant.

After years of losing touch with Chance, Neequaye and I
reconnected with him via Facebook. He was living in Phoenix
running his very own mobile dog grooming business, and with his
newfound freedom came wisdom that wasn't given, but earned.
Chance disclosed that he was HIV positive and from time to time

he struggled with depression, but he sounded happy. He confessed that he contracted the virus from John. Chance was planning a move to D.C., but didn't hesitate to give his two cents on Atlanta as he saw it after he moved away.

"Y'all girls in Atlanta aren't as progressive as you *should* be. It took stepping out of that bubble for me to see that all y'all seem to care about is who has on what, who's driving this kind of car and who's fucking who. It's sad. And, I'm so glad I'm not trying to be on the *A list* anymore just to get invited to a party."

Most of what Chance said I was feeling. I questioned whether short-lived relationships were endemic of Atlanta or if it was community-wide wherever gay men were. The easier it became to have sex, the more elusive love became, but I was unhappy living in Atlanta for reasons bigger than the drawbacks of the gay scene. I couldn't create because my mind was clogged with fear of not being able to survive financially day-to-day, thus creativity was blocked without a way to come through. I was too busy worrying to recognize the many *mini* miracles in my life that had pushed me forward. God was placing lily pads before each step I took. They didn't look stable, but they held me up until it was time to leap to the next one. God sustained me through the generosity of the people who appeared in my life.

My time in Atlanta was up, but fear paralyzed me. I was still convinced I needed to remain there to get my *big break*. I knew too many people and had a plethora of contacts there. Atlanta was the city where I had written music, developed a line of greeting cards that was carried in seven retailers, and the place *A*

Day in the Life was born. I talked myself into believing there were more reasons to stay than there were to leave.

I was comfortable, yet on edge in Atlanta. I grew accustomed to waiting for the next financial crisis to occur in my life. I wasn't breathing. I was slowly suffocating and the universe was squeezing the life out of me in an effort to force me out of Atlanta. It was the reason my car was repossessed, and it was difficult to pay the rent month after month. God was pinching me hard enough to make it too uncomfortable in Atlanta for me to want to stay. He was forcing me to leave, and I couldn't continue ignoring the signs.

In December 2010, I felt a tugging in my spirit. It was the first of its kind. I had never considered leaving Atlanta, but my instincts were telling me to move to Los Angeles. I came close to moving to New York when George Faison called and asked if I'd be interested in working with him on a show. George choreographed the stage version of *The Wiz* and won a Tony for his work. He said there was talk of staging a play based on E. Lynn Harris' first novel, *Invisible Life*. George wanted me to assist with the music that was being produced by Ashford & Simpson, but when the funding failed to come through I canceled plans to move.

I never had a desire to live in L.A., but I knew a seed was planted in me this time. I called two friends living in L.A. who had previously lived in Atlanta. I told them I was thinking about moving, and they encouraged me to put some serious thought behind it to make sure it wasn't a rash decision. I was planning to move because I had the nerve to believe God was telling me to go, not because it was impetuous. I prayed that if it was God's will for me to move to L.A. that He would make it a seamless process.

I began saving money and flew to L.A. in March 2011 to put things in motion. My nephew's cousin worked for an airline and the round trip plane ticket only cost me $100. During that trip, I secured a place to stay with a college friend's parents. They told me I could live with them rent-free until I found a job and enough money saved to move into a place of my own.

When I got back to Atlanta, I set my move date for April 28th so I'd be in L.A. for my birthday on May 4th. I hired a moving company to move my furniture from my apartment to Kencil's unfinished basement to store. Coincidentally, on the day the movers came, there was a yard sale in Kencil's neighborhood. Instead of having the mover's take my things to Kencil's, I had it transported to the yard sale. To my surprise, everything sold.

I waited a week before my move to call my nephew's cousin again to book my one-way flight to L.A., but he had been terminated. I was afraid to check the price for the flight because I knew it would cost a fortune. I thought I would have to push back the date to get an inexpensive flight. I reluctantly signed onto Delta's website to check the prices. The one-way fare was $127 including tax. I was ecstatic. I couldn't believe the fare was so cheap.

Just before I purchased the ticket, I recalled receiving a $75 travel voucher from Delta after writing a letter to customer service about a previous flight. In total, I paid $69 for my flight. It was meant to be.

Thoughts of leaving Atlanta made me very emotional. Despite the tough times I had, there were many fond memories, and I met some amazing people who I count as friends. I worried that we would lose touch in the way I lost contact with friends from college, but I knew this move was what I needed. Kencil reassured me we would never lose touch.

I packed my luggage in Kencil's car and we headed to the airport. I was in tears before we hit 85 South. I was leaving the place I called home for 13 years.

"You're just a plane ride away. I'll come there and hell, you can visit Atlanta. It'll still be here. You're young, and you don't have any kids. This is the time to do it. Baby live. This is gonna be good for you Craig. I'm not gonna cry. Unh onh. I'm not 'cause I know I'm gonna see you again. I'll miss you though," she said.

Kencil started out as my workout partner, but she became like a sister, mother, and spirit friend to me. Though she's fifteen years my senior, I could talk to her about anything and she never judged me. We taught each other about personal growth, and much about loving the people in our lives without fear of rejection. We laughed together and cried for each other when love didn't bloom in our lives or when we faced career lulls.

I jumped out of the car when we pulled up to grab my suitcase from the trunk of the car.

"Ok, Craig. You got everything?"

"Yea," I mumbled.

"Ok, give me a hug."

Kencil reached up for a hug and I could feel all of her weight on me. Her 5'6" frame felt like a ton of bricks weighing me down. She was crying.

"I'm gonna miss you so much. I love you so much. You're such a beautiful spirit."

"I love you too,"

"Ok, let me stop. I said I wasn't gonna do this."

I knew she would do it all over when she found the letter I handwrote the night before that I tucked in her lingerie drawer.

"Let me know when you make it," she said.

"I will."

I checked in and headed to the concourse train to my departure gate. When the doors of the train opened I saw Carrington.

"Hey, where you going?" he asked.

"I told you I was moving to L.A."

Over the years we stayed in contact, mostly because of his efforts, so we weren't completely out of touch. And, several of my friends were still his dental patients. He used his chair side conversation time with them to ask about me, and the things he didn't ask them he learned from my mother. Carrington continued sending Christmas gifts to my mom every year after we broke up, and she often reciprocated.

"You're leaving today?"

"Yep, today is the day. Where you going?"

"I'm going to Philly for a class."

"Oh, one of those certification classes?"

"Yea."

"Oh ok. How was Hawaii?" I said with a slight grin.

"Damn, how did you know I went to Hawaii?"

Two friends told me Carrington and Wendell were dating secretly. Well, at least they thought they were clandestinely. Apparently, they didn't want anyone to know because neither would own up to it, but they were spotted having dinner on Valentine's Day. I knew it was true because the two people who told me didn't know each other, and I learned from Lane that two people who don't know each other can't tell the same lie.

What I didn't tell him was that I overheard his boy toy telling Jamelle—my friend that owned the furniture store. I was on the phone with her weeks before and she happened to see Wendell in passing. I overheard Wendell telling her that he was just getting back from Hawaii with a friend. I put two and two together. I knew Wendell didn't have money to go to Hawaii unless the trip was sponsored, and I knew who sponsored it. Besides, Carrington and I had talked of going to Hawaii, but never made it there.

I wasn't bothered because I was over Carrington. It was typical Carrington style to be with someone who needed him financially to make it difficult for them to leave him, and Wendell's modus operandi has always been to find a man willing to provide because he didn't like to work nor did he have a clear career path in all the years I knew him. Wendell spent years bouncing from one *big* idea to another, so they were perfect for each other.

"You know Atlanta is small," I said.

Carrington realized if I knew he went to Hawaii that I also knew he was dating someone that was a friend of mine. This was my way of letting him know that I knew he was dating Wendell. What he didn't know was that I didn't care.

Before Carrington could probe me for answers the train stopped at the concourse for my flight.

"It was good seeing you. Take care," I said.

"Alright man. You too."

As I settled into my first day in Los Angeles, I got a text from Carrington asking the name of a restaurant my mom and I took him to many years before in Maryland when we were together. I knew it was just a *feeler* text. There was something else he really wanted to know, but he had to work his way up to it.

I kept it simple. I replied with the name of the restaurant and hit send. I didn't bother including any small talk. He responded, *"How did you know I went to Hawaii?"*

I never responded.

The closing doors on the train were symbolic of the final closure on that chapter of my life, and similar subterfuges in Atlanta.

PROLOGUE

I was involved briefly with a married man who believed he had the courage to leave his wife to be with me, and to live his truth. This isn't the typical story of a married man promising to leave his wife for a secret lover. Rather, this is a story, in part, about a gay man who *knew* he was gay before he got married, but chose to marry a woman because he didn't know how to break free.

Rocky and I met on a gay social media site three months after I returned to the east coast to live, and just eleven months after he was married. At the time we met, he was living and working in Dubai as a contractor for the government on a military base, while his wife was stationed in Tallahassee, Florida where they had a home.

In one of the first messages he sent me, Rocky shared that he was married, but that he had regrets. He explained that he had come out to his mother and siblings when he was eighteen years old. He sat them down one day in the family room and told them he was gay, but his mom struggled with the truth. In fact, the stress of Rocky coming out of the closet caused his mother's hair to fall out. Nevertheless, his first gay relationship ensued and lasted for ten years, but out of his family's sight in another state.

With his decade long relationship ending, Rocky accepted a job in the Middle East. It was in Afghanistan that he met his wife—a high-ranking officer in the military. Although he and his wife dated for four years before marrying, Rocky said that he was still romantically involved with men during the course of their engagement because his soon-to-be wife was a virgin. Rocky thought that he would be able to quell his attraction to men once he began having sex with his wife. However, one of the men he dated, for two of the four years that he and his fiancée were together, advised him against getting married because *he* had once been married himself, and he knew firsthand how Rocky's story would play out. He told Rocky that over time he would no longer be able to perform sexually, but Rocky ignored his advice and chose to get married with the hope that he could manage his desires for men.

Rocky had been molested as a child, so he was convinced that this molestation was the reason he was conflicted sexually, and he convinced his wife to believe the same. He believed God had answered his prayers by sending him a woman who could see beyond his past and accept him fully. However, Rocky hadn't been completely forthcoming with his wife about his relationships with men, and his past wasn't really in the past. Frankly, his future wife had no knowledge about his partner of ten years, who was also once married, or the three children that Rocky helped him raise.

Less than a year into his marriage, Rocky began to realize that the day would eventually come when he would leave his marriage because he fantasized about being with one man long-term. But, leaving his wife was never of urgent concern because he had yet to meet a man he cared enough about to walk away from his marriage. Instead, he would simply live on the periphery of the gay and straight worlds—bobbing and weaving between the two.

One month after Rocky and I began communicating over Skype, he started talking about leaving his wife for me, and I believed him. Rocky made a teary confession that, if we had met first, he would never have gotten married. Today, he's still locked in that marriage, pretending to be happy, pretending he isn't gay— even posting pictures of himself on Facebook with his wife to maintain the illusion because he fears disappointing his family by living in the light.

Rocky was a world away from me on the other side of the globe, so there was no immediate concern that I would, or even could, get tangled in his web of confusion because we were just chatting innocently—at least so I thought. We were separated by time and distance, but six months turned into six weeks, then six days quickly became six hours, six minutes, six seconds until we met for the first time face-to-face at Baltimore Washington International airport.

I never had any intention of getting involved with a married man or living in my nevers—doing the things I said I would never do such as participating in an abusive relationship, tolerating a cheating partner, or in this case getting involved with someone who was already in a relationship. What I know for sure is the moment we begin negotiating our *nevers* and compromising our standards is the moment we begin living in our nevers.

1 BEAUTIFULLY COMPLICATED

So much had happened in the three months after my ex, Jacob, and I broke up. I had lost faith in dating, in relationships in general, and I wasn't interested in getting to know anyone new on a romantic level.

I was living in Los Angeles, soul searching, still unsure why I had sold everything I owned of value to leave Atlanta, and move to a city where I knew only two people—and why I did so without a car or a job. Meanwhile, Jacob had moved to New York to build on a career as a magazine editor, and to create a new life with new memories to add to those from his grad school days at NYU.

Before Jacob and I ended our relationship, we talked about moving to Los Angeles together, but he later thought a move to New York would better suit us both professionally—he as an entertainment journalist and me as a playwright. Yet, there I was in Los Angeles, unsure what my next steps would be.

One week after our relationship ended, Jacob was offered an executive editor position at a national entertainment magazine. When he called to tell me the position he applied for before our relationship dissolved had come through for him in New York, I knew for certain there was no chance of salvaging the relationship.

When I saw his number flashing on my cell phone, I couldn't imagine why he was calling because we hadn't spoken in the week following the split. At the time, I was working part-time at my hosting job at Murphy's, a restaurant in the Virginia Highlands section of Atlanta. I answered his call despite the restaurant's strict no-cell-phone policy for employees. Leftover feelings from the break up gave me the courage to risk the penalty of answering his call. Frankly, I hoped that he was calling to say we'd made a terrible mistake by walking away from our relationship—that there was one more thing we could do to try to make it work. Instead, he was calling with his good news.

Jacob also told me on the call that it wouldn't be necessary for me to move my furniture right away from the West Midtown apartment we shared in Atlanta because he wouldn't be moving to New York for another month or so. I had moved out of the apartment two months before. My friend Kencil, who had been there for me countless times in the past, was there to pick me up, dust me off and give me a place to stay.

After Jacob's call, I felt empty and lost. It felt like we had broken up a second time. Jacob and I figured a position in New York would come through for him almost instantly because he had made a name for himself in Atlanta writing for such magazines as People, Vibe, InStyle, and Upscale. And, he was quickly outgrowing his positions at two national magazines, working as entertainment editor at one and managing editor at the other. But, for some reason, I never considered him leaving for New York so soon and certainly not without me.

After thirteen years in Atlanta, I craved a new beginning. I was beyond frustrated with my career and Atlanta's oversaturated gay scene that felt more like two degrees of separation rather than six. When Jacob told me about his new position, part of me believed he called only to rub it in my face because his competitive spirit could go from friendly to surly in the blink of an eye, and he knew how desperate I was to leave Atlanta.

In the weeks that followed our break up, I was flooded with thoughts about how things had played out between us. I was talked into a relationship with Jacob before I felt we had allowed adequate time to date. When I started going out with him, I was still recovering from the fiasco with Raylon, a guy I dated, who burglarized my apartment two years prior. When it came to allowing someone to get close to me, I was beyond cautious, even though I had known Jacob from a distance for years, and we shared a handful of mutual friends. I was still jarred by the experience with Raylon and slightly jaded.

Sure, I pursued dating Jacob initially. But, I entered into that relationship prematurely because I didn't want him to think I was still interested in dating other people or that I wasn't really serious about a commitment with him. The truth is, there were stages of development that we needed to reach before we graduated to the commitment stage, but we bypassed those and skipped steps.

On paper, Jacob and I were perfect—we made sense. We were both writers, we enjoyed traveling, discovering new foods and restaurants, and we had similar lifestyle interests. Nevertheless, we were different fundamentally, and I agreed to enter into the relationship before I was able to discover the vast differences that would ultimately cause the relationship to implode.

Jacob and I were seated at Rare, a tapas restaurant in downtown Atlanta, when he asked a second time, "Craig, what are we doing?" He was ready for the relationship, but I wasn't ready for a title—a commitment. After I explained why we weren't quite ready, he shut down. He sat quietly pensively until we finished dinner and the check came. Leaving the restaurant, I noticed tears in Jacob's eyes.

Technically, Jacob was already living with me in my Atlantic Station apartment because I usually picked him up from the airport when he returned from his press trips. But, I was still less than eager to call what we had a relationship. Eventually, I uncovered the reasons I was reticent to give all of my relationships a title. I prolonged the friendship phase, so that I wasn't required to do much heavy emotional lifting because I was intimidated by love, and the vulnerability that comes with being in love. It was a defense mechanism. I was afraid that we would fall into a routine or that we would become complacent. Simply put, I was scared that things would become stale and fall apart.

In hindsight, I realized my defense mechanisms were at play, an attempt to avoid heartbreak again—as in the case with my first love, Carrington. My instinctive reflex to guard my emotions could be compared to the way in which a muscle spasms in our back to protect the spine from trauma when involved in a car accident. Nevertheless, I agreed to be in the relationship with Jacob despite my insecurities.

Once our differences surfaced they knocked us off course and it was impossible to get back on track. Our respective lifestyles inevitably clashed as a result of toxic behavior that existed in each of us, and between us. Jacob's obsession to know it all coupled with his insatiable desire to have the last word contended with my internal battle with pride, ego and insecurities surrounding my career. At the time, I was unaware I still had those feelings looming.

Jacob had carved out an amazing career for himself, and I told him that often. He was up early most mornings writing stories for the two magazines he worked for and was out the door to meetings while I still slept or milled around the apartment trying to find my starting point. I was frustrated with myself and nervous that he would lose respect for me. I wanted Jacob to be as proud of the work I was capable of doing as I was of his work, but increasingly I shrank in our relationship. Oftentimes I shut Jacob out of my thoughts. Naturally, he took my silence personally and as a result gave me the silent treatment in return.

There was one particular aspect to Jacob's work that I no longer felt comfortable with, considering my circumstances. We would dress up several times a month in fancy clothes to dine on complimentary meals at expensive restaurants around town in exchange for a write-up in one of the magazines. Yet, at the time, I had difficulties managing my electric bill. Then there were the all-expenses paid getaways to quaint hideaway luxury boutique hotel properties. It was exciting at first, but it felt like I was playing charades because I was barely getting by. I was in the middle of a financial crisis. Yet, one weekend we drove a sky blue 2010 Phantom Rolls Royce to Charleston, South Carolina.

Every month I was delinquent with my rental payment, and although Jacob had gradually moved into my apartment, I couldn't bring myself to ask him for help paying the rent, and initially he didn't offer. Moreover, I no longer had the Honda Accord that my college friend Zoe graciously loaned me for six months after she relocated to Boston. She called to say her father would be taking over the car payments. Thus she scheduled a car transport company to pick up the car from Atlanta to deliver it to her dad in Michigan.

I felt unhappy and sad most times, but I refused to open up to Jacob about my financial challenges because there was an unspoken competition. He reminded me in a couple of our arguments that he paid for most of the things that we did. It was a truth that was hard for me to face.

Another issue was Jacob's unwillingness to fess up that his on-again off-again relationship with cocaine was back on. I wanted to believe him when he said he quit for good four months before we began dating. We were driving back from our first weekend getaway, a press trip to Tybee Island, when he told me he had quit. It wouldn't be long before I saw signs that he was still getting high. Frankly, I didn't really need tangible proof that he hadn't quit because on some level I knew intuitively. My eye was trained to spot a user from years of watching my sister battle addiction.

On two separate occasions, Jacob came in at 6 a.m., and I became more than eager to prove that I knew he was still addicted to drugs, while divesting my affection in the process. Our bond became a loveless, passionless relationship that ultimately taught me who I thought I wanted wasn't what I needed at the time—that the relationship was merely a bridge to the next phase of my life. Still, I would learn plenty from it about choosing a partner in the future.

There will be struggle in every relationship, but there should also be growth with struggle. Sadly, Jacob and I weren't growing together through our conflicts—we grew apart. We avoided the most important conversations at all costs—he, for the sake of maintaining the illusion of a picture perfect relationship, and I, for the sake of keeping the peace. Jacob and I avoided the tough conversations for fear of hurting each other, but our responsibility to the ones we love is to be open and honest—even if it hurts them.

Our job as a good partner is to be a mirror for those we love so they can see themselves through us. The issues that Jacob and I needed to sort through, we didn't; many things were left unsaid. Smaller issues went unresolved until they compounded into larger ones. The silence between us was louder than the things we said to each other and silence is what subsequently detonated our relationship.

One month into my move to L.A. I was still trying to convince myself that the breakup was best for both of us—we were too different fundamentally to be together. But it's not always easy to walk away from a relationship. Just when I was sure I was over Jacob I caught a glimpse of him in the audience of a VH1 Storyteller taping of a Maxwell concert. All of the feelings that I thought I had put away came crashing back all at once.

2 *LOST* ANGELES

I touched down in Los Angeles on April 28, 2011—six days before my 35th birthday. This move was a gift to myself. On the non-stop Delta flight from Atlanta, I promised myself that I wouldn't bring with me the fear and doubt that paralyzed me the last three years that I lived in Atlanta. In the weeks leading up to my move I prayed that God would connect me with people who know and love Him. I asked simply and emphatically that He repel evil, harm, sickness, disease and disaster. After all, I was moving to a city where earthquakes are commonplace. I had no idea what this move would mean for my life or what experiences were ahead.

After the flight landed, I grabbed my luggage from the carousel. My friends Dash and Dru, who I met in Atlanta, were parked outside of baggage claim waiting in Dash's Ford Explorer.

"Welcome to L.A., bitch!" Dash yelled.

"Heeey Craig!" Dru sang, while reaching for a hug from the passenger seat.

"How you feel?" Dash said looking back from the driver's side.

"I feel good. I still can't believe I'm here," I said.

"It's gonna take some getting used to," Dash answered.

"Hungry smurf, I know you wanna eat. I don't even have to ask that!" Dru said.

"Starving!" I agreed.

Dash and Dru were the only two people I knew in L.A. My college friends, from L.A. were now living on the east coast—one of them had helped secure a place for me to stay rent-free at her parents' home in the Crenshaw District of Los Angeles. Dash and Dru had accompanied me to meet Tori's parents, the Smith's, when I visited L.A. just before my move.

"Ok, we can go to Magic Johnson's TGIF in Ladera Heights," Dru said.

*****

Dash and I met in Atlanta, when I was 23, at our friend Gavin's barbeque. Gavin was a manager at Kenneth Cole in Phipp's Plaza. I remember the first time we met; Gavin offered me his 50% employee discount when I ventured into his store.

I had seen Dash at several of Gavin's past barbeques, but we never exchanged numbers. Our friendship was born after the *Lifetime* network aired the Robert Townsend film *Jackie's Back* starring none other than Jenifer Lewis. Dash and I knew most of the lines from the movie. The lines I forgot, he knew, and vice versa, but he didn't mind getting into character to act out the scenes in front of all of the guests at the barbeque. More than once, he provided the entertainment at Gavin's parties.

Dash was a character, but he definitely wasn't ensconced in the gay scene—he maintained a healthy distance to keep balanced. Eventually, Dash pulled away from Gavin and that crew partly because it was rumored that Gavin was pocketing the money we paid him for the shoes we bought at Kenneth Cole. The rumor was that Gavin was stealing the money because he would only accept cash, and there was no limit on the number of shoes we could purchase. Nevertheless, I owned a black lambskin blazer, and a closet full of Kenneth Cole shoes and boots.

One night at Club Fusion in Atlanta, I was about to hand my card to a bartender when he intercepted. He warned me not to use my debit card in a gay club.

"Bitch! What are you doing?" he hissed through his teeth.

"I'm getting a drink," I said slightly startled.

"You don't have cash?" he asked.

"No," I said.

"Then you don't drink! These kids would steal your fingerprint if they could!" he warned.

"What?" I asked.

"Bitch! …Child, three weeks from *tomorrow*, you wouldn't know what hit you! Them kids will go in that garbage can back there, get them carbons, and have a car in your name bitch! I've seen them do it! Bitch, I get nervous just being in the same room with some of these kids. I know them for their work. Child, they be using dead people's social security numbers to get apartments and shit. The *kids* are notorious bitch!"

23

I truly thought he was kidding.

"Stop playing!" I laughed.

"Tuh! Child, they'll steal your soul! Half these kids in here ain't saved!" he preached.

I swear Dash missed his calling as a comedian. He made the most serious things funny. Dash was six years older, and over the years he dropped many jewels of wisdom for me. He was the complete antithesis of Leslie, who was one of the first gay men to usher me into the gay community. Leslie had an agenda, and he showed me all the negative sides of the life, which left me skeptical of everyone. Dash's intentions were golden. He was someone I could look up to, and he often reminded me not to get lost in the life or the trappings of Atlanta.

Our friendship solidified on a weekend trip to Washington, D.C. for gay pride Memorial Day weekend in May 2000. Dash, a friend of mine named Neequaye and I flew to D.C. together. The three of us met one of Dash's closest friends who flew in to D.C. from Kansas City, Missouri, which was also Dash's hometown.

We reserved two hotel rooms in Crystal City, Virginia. Neequaye and I shared one room since we had been friends longer, while Dash and his friend shared the other. The four of us pitched in to rent a Chevy Blazer for the lineup of weekend events.

Dash towered over us, and looked more like our bodyguard. Dash stands about six feet four inches tall, and his weight has fluctuated since we met. At one time he worked out consistently with Neequaye and me in the gym, but fell off after getting down to his desired weight. He kept the weight off for a period, but slowly ballooned back to his original weight plus a few extra pounds.

Aside from the clubs every night there were picnics in the park, an all white attire party, and an impromptu invite from my mother to a family barbeque in Baltimore.

"Coretha is having a cookout Saturday. What are you doing tomorrow?" she asked.

My mom knew I was traveling to D.C. that weekend, and she was well aware that I was with some of my gay friends. Ironically, these were some of the same people she refused to meet when she visited Atlanta the previous Thanksgiving. I knew my aunt Coretha would be ok with my friends coming with me to her cookout because she had already embraced me in an unexpected letter she sent just after I came out, but my mom still hadn't shown any signs that she was ready to accept my gay friends.

"I don't know what we're doing just yet. But I can't just take the car and drive to Baltimore. I rented the car with three other people." I explained.

"Well, they can come too. Why can't they come with you?" she asked.

There was a brief silence. I wasn't expecting her to extend the invite to my friends.

"I'll ask them. I'll see what they say," I murmured.

My eyes met Dash's.

"We can go," Dash nodded.

Dash had never met my mother of course, but he knew my coming out story, and what had occurred with Saleem—the first man I loved after I came out. Once I trusted that I could tell Dash that Saleem was HIV positive, without fear of word traveling, I did. What I know for sure is gossip travels faster than good news, so I was very careful not to tell just anyone.

"Craig, this gay shit ain't no joke, bitch. It's a character builder. It'll either make you or break you," Dash offered.

His words were piercing. I didn't quite understand then why they felt so impactful, but I would understand in the years to come through my experiences dating, and my friendship with the Hettabrinks—my core group of friends at one point. We were named after the sisters from the television show, *Amen,* because we were all degreed, gainfully employed, independent, and single without any decent relationship prospects on the horizon. This life had made and broke some of us, without a doubt.

Dash and I had been friends for a couple years. For my 24th birthday, he hosted a birthday gathering for me and attempted to get Saleem to come, but he was a no show. Five months had passed since Saleem and I stopped seeing each other, and he was flaky at best in the remaining days that we spent together, so I knew without a doubt he wouldn't show up this time either. Saleem called to wish me a happy birthday, and after we spoke, Dash took over the call.

"Saleem why aren't you here? You know how much it would mean to Craig if you showed up," Dash said.

I couldn't hear Saleem's responses, but he obviously made up an excuse because the party ended and there was no sign of Saleem anywhere.

"You love that nigga, don't you Craig?" Dash said.

"Yeah," I smiled.

"Craig, what he look like? Is he fine bitch?" Dash asked.

"Oh, he's fine," I beamed.

After losing his job in Atlanta, Dash eventually moved to Dallas, which resulted in him selling his townhouse back to the bank as a short sale. He accepted a job with a major hotel brand that he enjoyed working with, but loathed his overbearing boss.

Although we were no longer living in the same city, we remained friends. I flew to Dallas to visit him the weekend before the 2007 production of my play, *A Day in the Life*, and when he came to Atlanta on a visit from Dallas, I introduced Dash to Dru.

Dash remained in Texas for about four years before relocating to L.A. to work with a skin care company. Now he and I would be living in the same city again.

Dru and I met through our friend Kimani when she first moved from L.A. to Atlanta six years earlier. Kimani was with me the night I chased Raylon through the streets of Atlanta with a carjack for stealing my clothes. Dru had moved to Atlanta to expand her image consulting business. For many years, she made a living booking hairstylists, make-up artists and wardrobe stylists to work with various celebrities.

After Dru's business folded, she made the difficult decision to leave Atlanta and return to L.A. to accept a job with her best friend, an up and coming actor/comedian. It was in L.A. that Dash and Dru cemented their friendship because true friends are hard to come by in L.A., and as they put it, "L.A. is no joke!"

Once I made the decision to move to L.A. I called Dash and Dru to share the news.

"Are you *sure* this is really what you wanna do? I only say that because if you're having a rough time in Atlanta, Craig, you may wanna really think about it. L.A. is *not* a game! It's hard out here and it's not easy to get connected to people. I mean, you have me and Dash, so that's a good thing, but at least in Atlanta you know people, Craig. You have a network to lean on there," Dru said.

"We don't wanna scare you, but bitch, you definitely have to be ready. Your money gotta be right. Shit is expensive here. Bitch, they charge extra for everything! Bitch, it's $8 for extra guacamole, and then you got crime!" he hollered.

"You stupid," I laughed. "I have thought about it, though. My *spirit* is telling me it's time to leave Atlanta and L.A. is where I need to be—I've prayed about it. This isn't a rash decision. I've actually been putting it off for a while," I said.

"Ok, well, if you prayed about it then go for it," Dru said.

*****

From L.A.X, the three of us laughed and talked on the way to dinner in Ladera Heights. Dru pointed out the Starbucks that appeared in the movie *Something New*, starring Sanaa Lathan, and I recognized Pann's across the street—the diner from the Tina Turner movie, where Ike wanted Anna Mae to "*eat the cake.*"

We got seated at T.G.I.Friday's and began talking the moment we sat down.

"So, you know I gotta take you to all the good food spots, bitch. There's this Thai place on Hollywood Boulevard—" Dash said.

"Is it good Dash?" I asked.

"BITCH! Is a pig's pussy pork?" he said fluttering his eyes.

"You a fool!" I said laughing hysterically.

"Dash, you are so stupid," Dru laughed, too.

"But wait, they have these Asian singers that work there. They be up on this little stage. Bitch—" he laughed uncontrollably.

Some of the other customers in the restaurant that were seated near us turned to look at us because we weren't using our inside voices.

"Dash, you so stupid. Finish the story!" Dru laughed, shaking her head.

"Bitch wait, they can barely speak English, but bitch, they be singing R&B songs with this little keyboard. Bitch, I was so weak the first time I heard them!" he laughed until his eyes watered.

"But can they sing? How they sound?" I laughed.

"For real, all jokes aside, they do sound good. Their lips just don't match the words," he laughed.

We ate and talked more about everything and nothing at all. We sat in the restaurant over two hours talking as if I was only in L.A. for a quick visit.

Dash and Dru took the liberty of filling me in on the differences between people from L.A., and people on the east coast. They advised me to take my time getting to know people since the City of Angels is known for opportunists and social climbers. According to them, people in L.A. aren't interested in genuine friendships; rather, they're looking for a chance to advance their own careers.

"If they think they can use you they'll keep you around. So, I don't fool with too many people out here. I have a handful of close friends—that's it," Dru said.

"Right, but if they can't use you for something, they ain't got time for you," Dash said.

"And be careful about what you say to people 'cause this industry is real small, and you never know who knows who. They're just real funny out here," Dru added.

"Mmmhmm," I said.

"Case in point, I was hanging out with this guy one day right? And he found out about a party while we were out—" Dash said.

"Uhh huh," Dru and I said in unison.

"So, he asked me if I wanted to go and I was like, 'yeah, that's cool.' So, he told me to follow him so we could meet a friend of his that was going. So, we driving and my cell phone rings and he's like, 'man, I'm not gonna go. I changed my mind,' but this motherfucker ended up going anyway. I found out later that the

dude we were following said something about what I had on,"
Dash explained.

"Huh?" I said.

"That doesn't make sense," Dru said.

"How did the guy know what you had on?" I asked.

"I'm sorry. I left something out. Ok, so, we met up with the guy that my friend knew on the way to the party. We were all in separate cars, so we just pulled up so we could follow the guy to the party, and he must've told the dude that I knew that he didn't like what I had on or something. He either called or texted him while we were driving," Dash explained.

"Well, what did you have on?" I asked.

"Bitch, come on. You know I had on some pieces. I mean, I was casual, but I never got out the car, which is my point, so he didn't know what I had on! He could only see my top half, and I had on a sweater. But, that's the type of shit they pull out here," Dash said.

"Wow, that's crazy," I said.

"Yeah, they do that. I'm not surprised," Dru said.

"Now bitch, I know you gonna make friends out here, and you gonna get invited to them industry parties. Just don't forget about your good girlfriend," Dash said.

"I got you!" I laughed.

Both Dash and Dru had been single for the better part of their stay in California, so they had even more to say about the dating scene in L.A.

"Black gay men out here are *such a disappointment*," Dash said.

"Why you say that? I thought L.A. would be different," I said.

"Yeah, ok! For one, most of them don't have their shit together," he said.

"How is it compared to Atlanta?" I asked.

"Bitch, in Atlanta at least the kids fool you into thinking that they have it together 'cause they got a car and an apartment. May not have no furniture in it, but they got a place!" he said.

"Right, with two, three roommates!" I laughed.

"—so they can drive a BMW," Dash added.

"Ok!" Dru laughed.

"'Cause the kids gonna give you some wheels. If they ain't got nothing else they got a car!" I said.

"And shoes bitch!" Dash added.

"I know that's right," Dru said.

"Out here, tuh, they're either sleeping on somebody's couch, don't have a job or a car, or they cheap as fuck! This one motherfucker thought I was gonna pay every time we went out to eat. Bitch! I ain't desperate! …The fuck I look like? I ain't paying for no dick!" he fussed.

"Child, I know that's right! But, honey the straight ones ain't no better! I'll be single forever out here! And the quality Black guys only seem to be interested in White or Latino women," Dru chimed in.

"Come on Dru! You better preach!" Dash cut in.

"But wait, Dash, and the Black men that do date Black women ain't about nothing," Dru giggled.

"Really? Are you serious?" I asked.

"Child, some of these Black kids out here don't even fool with other Black men. And bitch, they'll give you this look like they're better than you 'cause they run with these White children! Half of them Black kids won't even speak to you!" Dash said.

"Atlanta has definitely spoiled us as far as quality men go, but they got their shit too," Dash added.

"Child, it's just a mess either way," Dru said.

"Yea, the good ones know they're a commodity, so they play the field cause they know they don't have to settle down with just one person. But that's not just Atlanta, that's everywhere. It really is about connecting with someone who wants what you want when you want it," I said.

"Mmm, that's good Craig," Dru said nodding her head.

"Amen!" Dash said.

"I miss my life in Atlanta. At least I went on a few dates," Dru laughed.

I was slowly discovering the intrinsic bond between gay men and our female friends extend beyond the stereotypes surrounding our common interests in food, culture and fashion. Gay men and women suffer from the same trials, disappointments, heartache, and frustrations that come with dating and loving men—men are our biggest connection.

It was late when we finished dinner, so I called the Smith's to tell them I would wait until the next day to come to the house.

That first night in L.A., I crashed at Dru's two-bedroom apartment in the Valley on an air mattress in her spare bedroom.

3 HOPING FOR MIRACLES

My first priority once I got settled in L.A. at the Smith's house was to buy a car because public transportation wasn't as sophisticated or reliable as it was in most east coast cities. And, I knew that I couldn't rely on Dash or Dru to take me every place I needed to go especially since they both lived in the San Fernando Valley—Dash in Woodland Hills and Dru in Valley Village. I was centrally located in Mid-City, wedged between Baldwin Hills and Leimert Park. Still, one of the Smith's requirements to stay with them was to get a car.

Mr. Smith spent a few afternoons with me searching for a reliable car; however, the L.A. used car market was saturated with overpriced cars that littered the streets. My first choice was to purchase a pre-owned car from a private seller, but they all appeared to be junk cars. Even the late model cars were unappealing because they had substantial body damage, and mismatched or missing rims. Yet, the price tags on average were $500 more than they would've cost on the east coast.

So, I opted for a ten-year-old Honda Prelude that I saw online at CarMax because it was in mint condition—it had low mileage, an extended warranty, and most important the mile to gallon of gas ratio was excellent. At the time, regular gas in L.A. hovered at five dollars per gallon.

I had managed to put aside $1,400 from my part-time job in Atlanta, and profits from a yard sale in Kencil's neighborhood at which I sold everything. I planned to use most of the money for the down payment and car insurance. The only obstacle left was convincing my father to co-sign for the car since my candy-apple-red Acura had been repossessed, and my credit was still in shambles. But my dad wasn't exactly willing.

"Craig, I'm not co-signing for a car. You don't even have a job," he said.

"Dad, I'll get a job. I'll have a job before the first car payment is due," I promised.

I could hear my father breathing heavily on the phone. He was searching for a way out of the discussion. Convincing him to cosign would've been an uphill battle if he and JoAnne, his ex-wife, were still married, but then again I probably wouldn't have asked if they were.

"Ok, Slim," he sighed. "What you need me to do?" he asked.

"I'll call you when I get to the dealer. They'll need your social security number," I said.

"You know my social security number," he grumbled.

"Dad, I know, but I can't give it to them. And, they have to fax you some forms to sign," I explained.

"Craig, I don't have no fax machine!" he barked.

"Dad, I know you don't have a fax machine. You're going to the CarMax dealer there. The closest one to you is in Ellicott City. They'll have the forms when you get there. I'll let you know when to go, so they'll have them ready," I reasoned.

"Alright," he said.

Finding a job was the next item on my to do list.

Mr. Smith loaned me his laptop to apply for jobs online. I spent the first three weeks in my bedroom applying for jobs and registering with temp agencies with no results. The proverbial clock whose alarm would sound for my first car payment was ticking faster and louder with each passing day. I reminded myself that I hadn't moved to L.A. to panic.

All of the pieces necessary for me to relocate had aligned without force, including the one-way plane ticket I purchased for $69 one week before my move. Things had to work out. I left *fear* in Atlanta. I quickly reminded myself that I had the power to change my mind. I told myself, *something's gonna happen,* and quickly shifted my mind to something positive.

Nevertheless, I was reminded each time that I burned gas to follow up on a job lead, that I was 3,000 miles away from home. I discovered that I had to apply online—even for server positions at many of the restaurants. It was interesting that the restaurants required applicants applying for front of the house positions to upload a headshot with a resume. This was a different type of discrimination. They were looking to hire pretty people only.

Fortunately, I was still receiving my food stamp benefits from Georgia, so I purchased my own groceries and offered to share my EBT card with the Smiths, but they refused.

"We're old. We don't eat much," Mrs. Smith said.

Mrs. Smith asked often how the job hunt was going, and wasn't shy about telling me that she didn't think I was doing enough to find work.

"You have to pound the pavement. You can't stay locked up in that room all day on that computer. You have to go in person," she lectured.

"I've tried going in person. Most places don't even allow you to apply in person. It has to be done online—most jobs are like that. Some of the restaurants will let you come in to apply, but only at certain hours and I've done that," I explained.

"Yeah, they tell you that, but I'm old fashioned. You wait too late to go. You have to show some initiative. You need to be out there first thing in the morning," she said pointing towards the door.

"The times you can go are between noon and two—after the lunch rush, but before dinner," I advised.

"Mmmhmm," she hummed.

Mr. Smith, though, was a bit more relaxed with me. He was a spry 80 year-old man who still took flights alone to Vegas to bowl. I thought it was ironic that his wife was only in her 70s, but far more conservative than he.

It seemed to me that Mrs. Smith was searching for something else to say just to nitpick as older people do.

"Don't you get bored back there in that room?" she continued.

"No, I'm not bored. I don't have time to be bored. I have to find a job," I laughed.

"Half the time, I don't even know you're in there. You're so quiet," she said.

I tried to be invisible when I lived at the Smith's house because I recognized that I was no longer in my own space. I spoke in hushed tones on the phone, and tiptoed around the house at night if I was the last one awake. I never wanted to be a burden in any way and certainly didn't want to wear out my welcome. The only times I emerged from my bedroom was to eat or when Dash came by so we could hang out in West Hollywood. And every so often, Dru stopped by the Smiths to hang out until the traffic heading towards the Valley cleared up.

The Smiths spent most days at home watching television in the den. Mr. Smith played solitaire on his desktop, and some mornings Mrs. Smith took an exercise class, but without fail she attended the 8 a.m. service every Sunday at West Angeles Church. Sometimes she tried to convince me to go with her, but I never accepted the invitation. Occasionally the couple entertained a friend or relative, but they were mostly homebodies.

It was whimsical living in a city with tropical weather and palm trees lining the streets. Each time I caught a glimpse of the mountainous landscape floating by through the sunroof of my car, it seemed surreal.

"I live in L.A.," I said smiling to myself still in disbelief.

I never left the house without using the GPS on my cell phone to find my way around because on the few occasions that I stopped someone for directions, it wasn't a very pleasant experience. Seemed everyone was wearing an *I'm too busy to answer a question* look on their face—even when I stopped someone in standstill traffic. People just weren't very approachable and I got a sense of the coldness that Dash and Dru warned me about. It took about a month before I first attempted to drive someplace without using the navigation.

For a change of scenery, I sometimes ventured to the Valley to spend the day with Dru, but this didn't happen very often because the traffic in L.A. was too unpredictable, and I couldn't afford to burn gas on leisure trips. One afternoon at Dru's, we were both on laptops working while the television played in the background. Neither of us was really watching. The TV was just on to have sound in the room. VH1 was airing a Maxwell concert.

Dru was making phone calls and sending emails, while I was signing up with more temp agencies when I happened to glance up at the television.

"That was Jacob!" I said.

"Where?" she asked.

"In the crowd. The camera just panned the audience. He's sitting by the aisle," I said.

"I didn't see him. Was somebody with him?" she asked.

"That's what I'm trying to see," I said staring at the television without blinking an eye.

"Have you talked to him since you've been out here?" she asked.

"No, I haven't talked to him since I left Atlanta."

I was still watching for the camera to pass him again in the audience.

Truthfully, I hadn't thought much about Jacob once I got to L.A., but sometimes I was overrun with thoughts and memories that would push me to reach out to him, and toy with the idea of us getting back together. Perhaps things could be different.

There's a colorful story of compromises, obstacles, setbacks and other hurdles behind every long-term relationship. Certainly there were challenges along the way that weren't easy for Jacob and me to navigate, but I couldn't fathom why some couples were able to move past the very things that broke us up. But as my friend Kepri explained, *"You don't throw out brand new kitchen cabinets after you buy them just because they don't fit perfectly at first. You sand them down, make little adjustments, and re-hang them."*

Maybe it could work now because I was in a different frame of mind. Maybe this time, Jacob would be more interested in having a relationship than being right, because it's impossible to have both.

I thought back to when we started dating. I was out with friends, in Atlanta, at a club in Buckhead. I was seated near the exit because I was ready to leave, but my friends were still dancing. Jacob walked in and stood in front of me. He had just left a magazine release party that he hosted for one of the

41

magazines. I hadn't seen him since he sat in the audience of my play three years earlier. When he turned around, he saw me seated behind him.

"Hey, what's up, Craig?" he said leaning in for a hug.

He was wearing a blue and white-checkered button down shirt tucked in a pair of grey jeans, sans belt, and high top sneakers.

"Hey, how are you?" I asked smiling.

"I'm good—just working and traveling. That's about it," he said.

"Yea, I see your pictures on Facebook," I said smiling.

"What's going on with your play? I really enjoyed your show. It was really good," he said.

"Thank you," I smiled. "I'm looking for funding to get it up again. I wanna tour it. That's the goal," I said.

"You should. People need to see it."

"Yeah, I agree. It's hard getting funding though," I said.

"You know, I've interviewed a lot of celebrities and the one thing they all have in common is they never gave up. So you can never give up," he said.

"Yeah, that's true. I won't," I said smiling. "So, when are you gonna let me take you out?"

Jacob smiled and took a quick nervous look around the club as if someone may have been spying on our conversation.

"You're friends with my ex," he smirked.

"We're cool, but we're not friends. When I see him I speak, but we don't hang out. We don't talk on the phone. There's a difference," I reasoned.

"Mmmm," he said twisting his lips.

"He auditioned for the play. He was in my show. That doesn't make us friends," I said.

"Ok, where's your phone? I'll give you my number," he smiled.

"If things get serious between us, we'll tell him. I don't think he should find out from the streets," I said.

I pulled my cell phone from my pocket and stored Jacob's number, then texted him mine.

In the beginning, most of my calls and texts to Jacob were unanswered. He said it was because I caught him at the worst possible time in his life because he was really busy with deadlines for both magazines.

Eventually, I won him over and we started talking and texting each other every day, several times a day. It was easy for us to escape in the middle of the day for lunch because of the flexibility of his work schedule, and my lack of work.

"What are you doing Friday from 7 pm until Sunday about 4 pm?" he texted.

"Umm, all weekend?" I replied.

"Yeah," he typed.

"I don't know. Why?" I wrote.

"Can you make yourself available? I wanna take you somewhere," he typed.

"I can do that," I replied.

That Friday, we made the four-hour drive to Tybee Island. The tourism bureau in Savannah provided a beautiful three bedroom, two-bath beachfront condominium for the weekend. Jacob and I arrived on Tybee Island afterhours, so we picked up the keys to the unit from a rental office a few miles away from the condo. With the keys were instructions explaining how to access the unit from the elevator in the parking deck. There was one key to operate the elevator to gain access to the unit, and another key to enter the unit.

Once we stepped off the elevator we were standing in the living room. There was a flat screen television mounted on the wall with a full catalog of DVDs. The kitchen was in plain view and it was stocked with a full set of cookware, cooking utensils, and dinnerware, although we wouldn't make use of any of it because Jacob was given a full list of restaurants for us to dine in gratis for lunch and dinner by the tourism board.

That was the weekend that Jacob confessed, on the four-hour drive back to Atlanta, that he had used cocaine recreationally in the past. His admission gave me pause, and it foreshadowed the first crack in the foundation of our relationship that would continue to grow, and threaten to break us apart. I told Jacob that I was shocked because I had never heard that about him in all the years of knowing him.

I shared with him the story of my sister's journey with drugs and told him that I didn't have much tolerance for drugs because of that experience. I also explained my suspicions that Elden, one of the Hettabrinks, possibly used cocaine. I described how our friendship fragmented and subsequently ended as a result of his addiction with alcohol.

"Yeah, I've partied with Elden before," Jacob said casually.

Jacob wasn't using the word party literally, but figuratively. "Party" was code for drugs.

"Really? And I asked him if he was using coke, and he got offended that I asked," I said.

"I've partied with Julian too," Jacob added.

Julian and Elden were two of my closest friends at one point, along with the other Hettabrinks, Twiggy, DJ, Brent, Devon, Jude and Wendell. Their friendships carried me through my 20s. I never would have predicted that The Angels, *Charlie's Angels,* a subgroup of the Hettabrinks, comprised of Elden, Julian and myself, would be torn apart by substance abuse, among other things. But that's what happened.

I listened to Jacob talk about his experiences with my friends, experiences I had no idea about.

"Wow, now that's a surprise. I had no idea Julian was using too. Makes sense now, though. It explains why we all drifted apart and it wasn't just because our careers took us in different directions," I said solemnly.

No one lies to us more than we lie to ourselves. I used to lie to myself and say that we drifted apart because Elden's design firm business picked up considerably as did Julian's travel schedule with his job, but I knew better.

"No one has ever approached me with drugs," I said.

"That's 'cause they know who to approach. They already know who does it and who doesn't," Jacob said.

He explained that most of the guys in the clubs who got high did so in the bathroom stalls of the clubs, or at random after hour spots, undisclosed locations where just about any behavior was acceptable.

"So, how do you find out where the after hour is gonna be if the locations change?" I asked.

"In the club—someone will tell you before the club closes. *You* wouldn't know where these places are unless you're invited. They know *who* to invite," he said.

It was a secret world, much like the hidden cybersex community that I was once a part of, except they used code words for drugs like *molly* and *skittles* for ecstasy or *tina* and *bump* for cocaine or a drug to snort.

Worried now, I wanted to know more.

"So, how do you know you're done using?" I asked.

"I got tired of feeling the way I was feeling the morning after. And I looked around and didn't like the way I was living. I wanna live a certain way, and the people that were around me weren't really doing much. They weren't living up to their potential. I was the only one with a career at risk. They all had jobs," he said.

Jacob and I consummated the relationship the night we returned to Atlanta. He spent the night with me in my apartment for the first time, and never really left except to get more clothes from his parents' house. We were almost inseparable. We had our own language. If there were others around us, we had a way of communicating with one another without using words, and we laughed about whatever it was later once we were alone.

Initially, we both put forth effort to keep the other happy. While he was away on a weeklong press trip to Paris, I took the liberty of having a ding removed on the door panel of his C-Class, and had it repainted. I had a friend who managed the body shop at a Lexus dealer, so he did the work for me as a favor.

Jacob went out of his way for me time and again, either by assigning a story for me to write for one of the magazines to put money in my pocket, or by getting my expenses covered to travel with him on most of his press trips.

Despite it all, deep down I knew reaching out to Jacob from L.A. to revisit the past was pointless because we had tarnished things beyond repair, and more importantly our personalities clashed. Although there was now time and space between us, people never really change—we only get better at hiding who we *really* are. But, I reached out anyway.

Again, Jacob ignored most of my calls and texts like he did in the beginning, but I suspected it was intentional this time, and not because of a hectic work schedule. When Jacob did reply to my messages, his responses were brief, and he evaded certain texts that I sent him.

I searched his Instagram and Facebook pages for clues to determine if he was dating someone new, but there were no pictures or posts that pointed to a relationship on the horizon. There were indications, however, that led me to believe he was still having a really good time drinking, and dibbling and dabbling with drugs. In some of his pictures on social media, there was a vacant look that hazed Jacob's eyes. Seeing those photos helped me realize that I wasn't craving to be with Jacob after all. Rather, I was feeling lonely and a bit nostalgic.

I snapped out of my daydream when Dru's cell phone rang. I packed up Mr. Smith's laptop, and headed back over the hill.

*****

It came as shock when Mrs. Smith announced that she had family coming for a visit in July, two months away, and they would need to stay in the room I was occupying.

"We have family that comes every summer for a month. I wasn't expecting it to take this long for you to find a job and get a place of your own," she said softly.

It's only been three weeks, I thought to myself.

"I think you may have come to California at the wrong time. You may just need to go back east," she said.

Even if I had landed a job my first day in L.A. I would've still needed more time to save the security deposit, and the first month's rent because that's what's required in L.A. For Christ's sakes, I had just bought a car. *How much more was I supposed to accomplish in three weeks without a job?*

"We can give you until the end of May, but you'll have to find someplace else to stay. Do you think one of your friends will let you stay with them?" she asked.

There were only 8 days left in the month when Mrs. Smith dropped the news on me.

"I don't know. I can ask Dru, but Dash rents a room in a house, so that's not possible, He doesn't have space," I said.

I was almost in shock. *What am I going to do with this car?* Had they told me when I visited they were only giving me a month to stay with them, I would never have moved across the country. Finding a job was proving to be more challenging than I expected because the economy was still in a frenzy from the crash of the housing market.

"Y'all are friends right? I can't understand why a friend wouldn't let you stay until you can get on your feet," she rambled.

"I'll have to ask."

"We've done everything we can to help you," she said.

"Ok, I understand," I mumbled.

Mrs. Smith moseyed out of the kitchen and back to the den. I was left wondering how this dilemma would play out. My mind was scrambled. I couldn't think. I called Dash and recapped what happened.

"What?! Did you call your mother?" he asked.

"Hell no. I don't need her worrying," I said.

"Have you called Dru?" he asked.

"Not yet. I called you first. I had to vent. I can't believe this shit," I said.

"So, they never said they were only giving you a month?" he asked.

"No! I wouldn't have brought my ass out here for thirty days. All they said was, 'Find a job and get a car. You can stay until you get a job and save the money to move out.' That's it," I explained.

"Damn. That's crazy. What kinda shit is that? Well don't stress about it. We'll figure something out. Even if you have to come over here and sleep in this bed with my big ass for a while," he said.

"Alright, let me go," I sighed.

I hung up with Dash and called Dru. Again, I recited the conversation that I had with Mrs. Smith verbatim.

"See! I told you L.A. was hard! What you gonna do, Craig?" she said.

I couldn't believe her first words to me. There was no compassion, empathy or sensitivity. I had planned to ask Dru if I could crash at her place until I figured out my next move, but her reaction thwarted my attempt. I never anticipated an extended stay with Dru because she wasn't in the position to carry anyone, but I assumed that, as my friend, she would offer me a place to sleep even if only until I could scrape up enough money to buy a plane ticket to fly back east.

"I don't know. I gotta figure something out," I said.

"Umph mmm. They didn't tell you this before you came, Craig?"

"No, you think I would've come out here if I knew this?" I asked rhetorically.

"I just can't believe they didn't tell you. What happened, Craig? Did something happen that you're not saying? This just don't sound right. Ok, Ok, tell me exactly what she said," Dru said.

"Nothing happened. They just told me last week how quiet I am, and how they barely know I'm here. She just told me that she thought I would have a job by now," I whispered.

The Smiths were two rooms over in the den, and I didn't want them to overhear what I was saying.

"So what you gonna do? Where you gonna go?" she asked.

"I have no idea," I said.

As we talked, I thought to myself, this can't possibly be the same person I cooked for on a few occasions, when her money was too tight to buy groceries, or to eat out when she was struggling to hold on to a fledgling business. And, when I was flying high, I had even invested $2,500 in a business idea she had.

"Well, how much money do you have saved? I can ask around to see if someone has a room for rent. They usually go for about $500 a month depending on where it is," she offered.

"I don't have money to rent a room. I don't have a job, and I just bought that car," I snapped.

"See, this is why I kept telling you to make sure you could handle moving out here," she said.

"You're saying that like I knew this would happen. This was an unforeseen circumstance," I said.

"Well, see if they'll let you stay a little longer. Did you ask?"

"No, I'll figure it out. Let me go. I need to make a call," I said.

I was reminded on that call that friendship is a responsibility that isn't always convenient nor is it always reciprocal, but there should be balance. It was clear that my friendship with Dru was out of balance.

Fortunately, I had begun learning to panic less about things I have no control over. I had become more settled in crisis because of past experiences. Somehow I managed to relax because it *felt familiar in ways*, and on some level deep down inside *I knew* I would get through that moment.

Before I moved to California, my friend Gabby, whom I met on a visit to L.A., suggested that I connect with her hairstylist friend Chaz when I got settled, so I sent him a text.

"What's up Chaz? It's Craig. I'm a friend of Gabby's. She gave me your number to reach out once I moved to L.A.," I wrote.

"Hey man. Yes. How are you?" he replied.

"I'm ok. I'm trying to find work. If you hear of anything would you keep me in mind?" I messaged.

"Ok, what do you do?" he wrote back.

"At this point, anything. I'm actually looking for a place to stay too. I just found out that I have a week left at the place I'm staying," I typed.

My cell phone rang. It was Chaz calling.

"Hello," I said.

"Hey, what's going on?" he asked.

"Hey...how you doing?" I said forcing a smile.

I was glad that he'd called so suddenly.

"So, what happened?" he asked.

I explained my situation to him.

"I came out here a few weeks ago from Atlanta. I'm staying with a friend's parents. Originally, they told me I could stay until I found a job, but they just told me today that I have until the end of the month."

"What area do you live in?" he asked.

"I'm in the Crenshaw District—off 39th and Buckingham," I said.

"Ok, I live right around the corner from there. My place has two bedrooms, but my mother stays with me 'cause she had a stroke a couple years ago, so she's in a wheelchair. But you're welcome to stay with me as long as you need," he said.

"Are you serious?" I asked.

"Yeah, it's no problem. I was homeless before. I didn't have anywhere to go and my family was right here in L.A. I don't mind helping anybody."

"Wow, I really appreciate that. I don't know when I'll be able to pay you anything, but I get food stamps, so I can buy the groceries," I said.

"That's fine. At least you're offering that. I had a friend who stayed with me an entire year and didn't even offer to do that. But, I'm at the shop so just let me know when you wanna come," he said.

"Ok, it won't be today. I'll stay here until the end of the month, but I'll let you know when I'm coming."

"Ok," he said.

"Thanks again," I added, grateful for his offer.

"No problem. I'll talk to you later."

I don't know if I was more stunned that a complete stranger, someone I had never met or spoken to, offered me a place to stay, or livid that Dru hadn't. Still, there's reason for everything. It all had purpose, and with every step of faith that I took for myself, God moved me three more.

I appreciated Chaz's offer, but I wasn't in a rush to move in with someone I didn't know. Since the Smiths were giving me another week, I waited—anything could've happened before the end of the month. Perhaps, a miracle was just around the corner.

4 FRIEND OF A FRIEND

My friend Tori called frequently when I was staying with her parents to see how I was adjusting to L.A. She thought it was hilarious that I was rooming with her elderly parents and sleeping in her old bedroom, but glad to be able to help with my transition to the west coast. I noticed that her calls tapered off around the time her parents asked me to leave. I called her to tell her that she didn't have to feel bad that things didn't work out—that it was no fault of her own. We both agreed that her mom had an unrealistic timeline in mind for when I would get a job, and a place of my own. More importantly, I didn't want Tori to try to sway her mother's decision since I had found a place to go.

On the last day of May, I began packing all my belongings into my car to leave the Smith's house to move in with Chaz. I spoke with Dru sporadically the last week that I spent at the Smith's. She said she was calling to see how I was making out, and if I had found a new place to stay, but she never offered me the empty bedroom in her apartment. I told her that a friend of a friend was allowing me to stay with him.

Although Dru and I attended her church a few more times together, I had already begun re-categorizing our friendship, and her place in my life. I slowly began distancing myself because I didn't have room in my life for anyone posing as a friend, especially if they were no longer bringing value into my world.

Chaz texted me the address to the salon he was working for on Pico Boulevard because he still had a few more clients to finish before he left work that day.

I called Dash from my cell phone as we drove to the salon. Dash met me at the Smith's house and followed me to the salon. Though I had misgivings about telling him the story, I couldn't resist talking about my disappointment with Dru.

"I still can't believe Dru didn't even offer to let me stay with her. And I'm not saying it's her obligation because that's her apartment and she's not responsible for me. It was my decision to move here, but you mean to tell me she couldn't say, 'Craig, you know I don't want a roommate, but I can give you a month to figure out what you're gonna do,'" I said.

"Did you ask her if you could stay?" Dash asked.

I could tell from Dash's tone that he didn't want any part of this conflict. He was trying to play Switzerland and remain neutral to prevent pissing me off by choosing Dru's side, but I knew Dash well enough to know that he was partial, and the pendulum wasn't swinging in my favor.

"No, I didn't get a chance to! The first thing she said when I called was, 'See I told you L.A. was hard!' She made it impossible for me to ask. And again, I don't want you to walk away from this conversation hearing me say that she had to open up her place to me. But you and I know damn well that if I had a two-bedroom apartment with an empty bedroom, and one of you found yourself in a predicament like this, if I didn't offer you a place to stay, but said, 'What you gonna do?!' you both would call me all kinds of selfish motherfucker!" I snapped.

"Yeah. You right. That's true," he said.

"I know I'm right! But a complete stranger opened up his place to me. Someone I've never met in my life. A stranger! Yet, she's parked in church every Sunday. But, it's ok. Tables turn. And they *will* turn," I said.

After inadvertently passing it, Dash and I finally pulled up to the salon. The tiny salon, a block from Roscoe's Chicken & Waffles, was situated in a strip with mom and pop shops, and a few nondescript buildings. We walked up to a white wrought-iron gate. The peeling paint on the door revealed rust, which suggested the business wasn't well maintained.

A client opened the door after I banged on the wrought-iron gate twice. My heart danced with nervousness. I still couldn't believe I was about to move in with someone I had never seen before. Once the door opened, I could see the entire salon in one sweeping glance. It was narrow and reminiscent of a shotgun house. There were five hairdressing stations. All of the stations were empty except the one where Chaz was working.

Chaz was medium build and average height. He was bi-racial, mixed with Black and Mexican, so I was unsure if his fine jet-black hair was natural or dyed.

I walked over to Chaz's station.

57

"How you doing? I'm Craig. This is my friend Dash," I smiled slightly.

Chaz was still holding a pair of steaming hot hair curlers when he greeted us.

"Hey, how you doing? Nice to meet you," he said with a smile. And then to Dash, "What's up?"

"Ehh, what's up man?" Dash answered with a fist bump.

Beneath Dash's machismo was a softer side. Dash reserved virility for straight or gay men that he didn't know, but with women and others he knew well he showcased a more comfortable side of his true personality. Since Dash didn't know Chaz he butched up a bit.

Chaz was handsome, and his teeth were perfectly veneered. He was dressed comfortably in a denim button-down shirt, and cargo pants with sneakers.

The salon was practically empty, but there was music playing from a small portable radio. There was one person in Chaz's chair, and the girl who answered the door was seated on a black faux leather couch that was peeling just as much, if not more, than the wrought iron door. If the salon was any indication of where Chaz lived, I would be leaving L.A. sooner than I anticipated.

I replayed an imaginary scene in my head of myself returning home to Baltimore to start over. After all, home can be good sometimes. But, I knew my time in L.A. wasn't up. I could see far better days on the horizon. Something better was coming, I just knew it. I imagined a life of purpose, and imagination is God's way of showing us a preview of what's possible in life.

"Where you move from?" Chaz asked.

He was still pressing his client's hair, blowing softly on the hot curlers and talking to us simultaneously.

"Atlanta, but I'm from Maryland," I answered.

"I thought about moving to Atlanta, but Atlanta is too much for me. Unh onh, I was scared to go there," he said.

"What you mean?" I smiled.

Chaz laughed.

"There's too much going on there."

Then he turned back to Dash.

"And where you from?"

"Kansas City, Missouri," Dash responded.

"You just moved here too?" Chaz asked.

"No, I've been out here for a while," Dash replied.

Dash was careful never to divulge too much too soon to anyone, especially one of the kids. He wasn't one to give out too many specifics about where he worked or lived. It was his way of keeping *the messy kids* out of his personal business.

"So, how do you know Gabby?" Chaz asked.

"I met her a couple years ago when I came out here to shop a TV show with Dwight, from *The Real Housewives of Atlanta*. She and I met at DIVAS Simply Singing," I said.

"Oh, Ok. She's one of my clients. I love her," Chaz said.

"Yea, she's a sweetheart," I agreed.

"We can leave in a minute. I'm almost finished," Chaz continued blowing his client's hair dry.

"Ok," I said.

Dash and I retreated to the shabby couch and took a seat.

After his last client, Chaz switched off the radio and lights and went around to lock up the salon. He told us he was parked in the rear parking lot, so Dash and I pulled our cars around to the back of the salon so we could follow him to his house.

As we left the salon, Chaz mentioned that two of his friends were visiting for the week from Portland, Oregon. He said they were sleeping in his living room on the floor and couch, so I could sleep *with* him. I didn't know what to expect. I was grateful for Chaz because he didn't have to welcome me, a total stranger, into his home. I was clear about that, but I was also humiliated to sleep in a bed with someone I still didn't really know.

I felt foolish for believing that God had instructed me to move to a city that was foreign to me, aside from three visits. I wanted to believe there was some light at the end of a seemingly dark tunnel, which was my life. The glint of light that I squinted to see was extinguished instantly with the thought of the car payment that would soon be due.

The three of us caravanned to Chaz's place—Dash followed behind me in his own car to see where I'd be staying, and to be there with me for moral support. My cell phone rang shortly after we pulled away from the salon.

"What's wrong?" Dash asked.

"I can't believe this shit," I mumbled.

"Well, he seems cool," he said.

"Yeah, he does," I agreed reluctantly.

The streetlights flickered as we passed the Baldwin Hills Mall. It appeared that we were approaching Baldwin Hills, a community that was known at one time to be the home of L.A.'s Black elite, but we stopped in an apartment community just below the development. We were within a five-minute drive from the Smith's well-manicured neighborhood, but such wasn't the case for this apartment community. It was a low-income housing project—also known as The Jungle. This was a depressed community with graffiti sprayed along the walls of some of the surrounding buildings. There were abandoned homes close by and storefronts that appeared to have been closed for decades.

Chaz pulled his white Porsche Cayenne into a dark alleyway to park behind his apartment quad. Meanwhile, Dash and I parked on the street. Dash pulled beside me and lowered his passenger window.

"You okay?" he asked.

"I have to be," I said.

"All right, I'm about to head home. That drive ain't no joke. I just wanted to make sure you got here. I'll call you tomorrow," he said.

"Ok, thanks Dash. Text me when you get home," I said.

"Alright. Bitch, don't leave nothing in that car and make sure you lock them doors," he said.

"Yeah, I will," I laughed.

Dash had become an unofficial financial support system for me once I moved to L.A., and I felt indebted to him and other friends who fed, sheltered or gave me money. I felt even more indebted to Chaz because I didn't know him at all. But, I remembered I had been that sort of friend to others at one time or another.

On two separate occasions I opened my home to friends in Atlanta who found themselves displaced. But in my own case, I found it a bit unsettling living under someone else's roof. It brought on feelings of inadequacy, insecurity and moments of weakness that fed deep-seated fears and created self-doubt. Some way, somehow my self-worth was attached to the feelings I had about my position in life at that time. But, moments of weakness don't make us weak—they make us human.

Chaz was waiting for me by the back gate of the quad. There were about twelve units in total. Toys littered the courtyard, which indicated there were plenty of children who lived in the neighborhood. It was well into the night, and I could hear people talking, either on telephones or face to face. Television noises came from multiple units as we walked to Chaz's apartment.

I wondered what all this would mean for my life in the greater context. The road in front of us has to have twists and turns. Otherwise we would run straight for the goal without making any detours—ultimately bypassing the pit stops—the places of wisdom that God *gifts* us along the way. *What lessons was I supposed to learn from this experience?*

I knew one day this would all make sense to me, because even setbacks are a part of the fabric of our story. I figured the lessons I learned would be difficult because growth is painful, but somehow I knew that if I could stick it out in California, peace of mind was on the other side of my sacrifices. I only wondered what I was willing to sacrifice to grab hold of it.

5 THE JUNGLE

Chaz shared his bed with me the first week while his friends were in town visiting. He remained on his side of the bed, and I slept close to the edge on my side. I didn't want to take up too much space, nor did I want to send any mixed messages.

I lived out of my suitcases, which I kept at the foot of his bed because there was no closet space for my things. In total, there were five adults sharing one bathroom, and a handful of bath towels. Chaz's houseguests returned to Portland a week after I moved in, but it was agonizing trying to get into the bathroom before they left.

By mid-June, I was no longer sleeping in the bed with Chaz, but in the living room on an air mattress. Sleeping in the middle of the living room left no privacy because I was exposed to everyone who passed through including his brother who visited his baby's mother, who lived in the apartment below us.

Every morning I was awakened by children screaming in the courtyard, screen doors slamming shut, arguing or yelling coming from the other units, or the summer heat because Chaz's apartment didn't have central air. There was a single window unit and it was in Chaz's bedroom, which he locked each morning before he left.

Chaz's mother was an ornery woman, and made no apologies for being snappy whenever she talked to me. She was a fair-skinned woman who could pass for White, but her mixed silver and black hair pointed to her Black and Mexican heritage.

Her twisted lips were evidence of the stroke she had suffered three years before. Although she was in a wheelchair she was able to walk—she just wasn't comfortable doing so after a fall, which resulted in a broken hip. Instead of walking she chose to use her feet to scoot herself around the apartment in the wheelchair.

Ordinarily, she would simply pass me in her wheelchair without saying anything to me. The only time she addressed me was if we were the only two in the apartment, and she needed me to do something that she was unable to do for herself—and even then she never made eye contact with me. It was no secret that she didn't like me, or the idea of me staying at the apartment.

Every morning, without fail, Chaz's mother would be in the bathroom an average of forty-five minutes—leaving me no option, on a few instances, but to pee outside on the backside of the building. And, when I was finally able to get in the bathroom, I hated using it because it was less than presentable. Before I could use the toilet I had to remove the assisted toilet seat that lived over the toilet because Chaz's mother used the safety railings to sit down. I hated touching it even to remove it because it was cruddy, and in need of a good cleaning.

The shower didn't seem to get much use by Chaz or his mom. Unfortunately, she relied on him to bathe her, but I only witnessed him bathing and changing her pajamas about once a week. And if she had street clothes, I never saw them because she never left the house. So she wore the same dingy nightgown every day.

When I showered, I noticed his mother's long stringy hair clogged in the drain—causing the water to fill up around my ankles. After every shower I carefully stepped out onto a towel so that I could rinse my feet and ankles under the running water one at a time. I was completely miserable living at Chaz's. I struggled to find the balance between gratitude and wanting more for myself.

Chaz usually left first thing in the morning to head to the salon, but I would later discover that he was leaving to escape his mother—he didn't have very many clients. He spent most of his days running around L.A. visiting people he knew. Chaz primarily supported himself with his mother's monthly $1,700 social security disability check. With her money, he paid the rent and the $600 monthly car payment on his Porsche truck.

Chaz's mom called him incessantly, but he avoided most of her calls. At times, he had ten to fifteen voice messages from her in a day. Usually, she was calling to ask him to bring something to eat because he never cooked. Typically, he brought her fast food at the end of the night.

Fortunately, I still hadn't canceled my food stamp benefits, and could buy hot food in L.A. I was using my EBT card to eat out even after I bought groceries because I refused to use the dishes and silverware in the apartment. They were covered with a sticky dust residue because no one used them regularly.

It became difficult for me to ignore Chaz's mother once she cursed at me and called me stupid. Her repugnance caused me to snap back at her a few other times when she was unceremonious with me. I was tired of being affable, and I began to ignore her when she called for my help with whatever she needed at the moment.

My father had practically begged me not to move to California, so I didn't bother telling him that I was having a rough time, because I knew he would tell me to pack up and come home. When my mother asked how things were going at Chaz's, I told her how cantankerous Chaz's mom was, and that I began ignoring her because of it.

"I'm really ashamed at you," she said.

"What? Why?" I asked.

"Cause you know better. I don't care what she's doing or what she says. She's confined to that wheelchair, and you said yourself that she never gets out of that apartment. It's all hot and stuffy in there. What kind of life is that? You have to consider all of that. How would you feel if you were in her position?" she lectured.

Chaz had three siblings, but none of them seemed to have a hand in his mother's care. I met one of his sisters when she brought her baby over one afternoon. And of course, there was his brother who barged in either before or after visiting his child, but their oldest sister never came around.

I later suggested an adult daycare program to Chaz because my mom owned an assisted living business and she utilized an adult daycare program for her clients. But Chaz dismissed the idea saying the pickup schedule conflicted with his work schedule. I was careful not to push the issue because I knew how sensitive it can be with regards to personal family issues, and I didn't want Chaz to think I was criticizing how he cared for his mother.

My mother had a point. I hadn't really considered how his mom felt being left unattended with a stranger. I was a stranger to her. His mom and I were lashing out at each other because of our respective circumstances.

I guess I believed Chaz when he said she was self-sufficient, but she really wasn't. On a few occasions, he had to clean her up after she had an accident on herself.

During that conversation with my own mother, she reprimanded me for my behavior.

"You change the way you speak to her. I don't wanna hear no more about you mistreating her. You know better than that."

My mother was right and there wasn't anything I could say, so I listened.

After we hung up, I called my cousin Tiffany to complain to her because I deserved some sympathy too, but she wasn't handing out any either.

"If you can't handle it, go home. You don't have to be there. Pack up your stuff and go back to Baltimore," she said.

Tiffany was still living in Cleveland, Ohio. I knew I could always get sound advice from her even if it wasn't what I wanted to hear. She was the one family member who had nudged me to come out of the closet before I came out.

"Nooo, that's not what I'm saying," I whined.

"Well, what *are you* saying? That's what I'm *hearing*," she said.

I was almost embarrassed to say it—ashamed even.

"It's the *projects* Tiffany," I said with my teeth clenched.

"You used to stay down at mama's house! What's the difference?" she said.

"That wasn't the projects," I said.

"It was still run down! They had roaches, and barely had hot water—it was always off! Boiling pots of water just to take a bath. Come on now, they had holes all in the walls—using cardboard or newspaper just to close the front door. So, what are you saying? You too good now?" she rambled.

"That's not what I'm saying Tiffany," I laughed. "You make me sick," I continued.

"You have to find one thing to be grateful for every day. One thing, everyday!" she said. "Change the way you look at things," she added.

After speaking to my mother and cousin, my insensitivity left me abashed. There were blessings in every single day. I could have been sleeping in my car. I began counting my blessings every day from that day forward, and realized I had a list of things for which to be grateful. It was up to me to notice them. It was just a matter of perspective.

Once my perspective changed about my living conditions, I felt a shift. The shift wasn't immediate, it was gradual, but I felt a change of energy. I slowly taught myself a lesson in adapting to whatever came. There's an art to knowing when to yield and when to proceed, and when to zig and when to zag.

I decided to turn over a new leaf. Whenever I left the apartment, I told Chaz's mom that I was leaving so she was aware that she would be alone, and when I returned with food for myself I brought food for her too. Even after I began sharing my food with her, she was still crabby with me, but I overlooked it, and simply asked her where she wanted me to set up her plate.

Gradually, she started opening up to me. I heard her laughing for the first time.

"What's funny?" I quizzed.

She was so tickled that she could barely explain the joke through her giggles and stutter.

Chaz's mom was also a recovering drug addict, and I believe the stuttering and her tendency to repeat herself were symptoms of years of abuse. Chaz told me during the time that he was homeless his mom was unavailable because of her drug use.

"I don't know why I didn't like you. I didn't like you, I didn't like you. I just didn't like you," she chuckled.

"I don't know either," I said smirking.

"I don't know why I didn't like you. Didn't like you. I didn't like you," she repeated.

"Yeah, you were mean to me for no reason," I smiled.

"I'm sorry. I'm ssss...sorry," she stuttered and laughed.

"It's ok," I replied.

After a little kindness, she knew I wasn't her enemy and I knew she wasn't mine.

*****

Despite what most people believe, there isn't much of nightlife in L.A. Most of the restaurants, bars and clubs close relatively early, so we were always looking for a new adventure. Chaz, Dash and I had the crazy idea of dressing up to go on the television show, *Let's Make a Deal*. We were all equally stunned when Wayne Brady called Dash up, and even more shocked when he won $1,000.

Because the job market in L.A. was pretty dry, in the beginning game shows and casting calls became my way to make money. Chaz also connected me with one of his clients who paid me $1,000 to research some information for her Hollywood producer husband. The money came just before my first car payment was due. I paid my cell phone bill, and made two car payments.

The three of us rendezvoused in West Hollywood, known also as WeHo, several nights a week, and again on weekends, looking for things to do. Chaz's place became our meeting spot so Dash could park his gas-guzzling Ford Explorer, and because parking in the city is a nightmare, especially in WeHo.

The gay nightlife in L.A. was denser because it lacked variety. I craved more urban music to be woven into the club music, but unfortunately what was considered *hip-hop music* at the clubs in West Hollywood didn't even come close. And, the clubs that did play hip-hop music were slipshod, dark, dank or run down, like The Catch One.

We hopped in Chaz's Cayenne and sped down Pico to Redondo then to San Vicente and Melrose en route to The Abbey on Robertson. We always parked on a side street a few blocks away from The Abbey to take a gander at Santa Monica Boulevard.

Chaz spoke to several people standing along the street as we strolled past Fiesta Cantina and Mother Lode. Gabby told me, before she gave me Chaz's number, that he knew everyone in L.A., and it was obvious that he was pretty popular on the strip. He even stopped to have conversation with a few drag queens, which prompted me to exchange a few clandestine glances with Dash.

Once we were seated at The Abbey, Chaz proceeded to tell us that most of the people he chatted with he didn't know—they knew his alter ego Jennifer. He told us that he kept his costumes and wigs in the garage behind his apartment. No sooner had he said it, than Dash hit me under the table and bit his bottom lip to keep from laughing. Chaz wasn't just a hair and make-up artist. He also moonlighted as a drag performer and had a cameo in an episode of the short-lived Logo series, *Noah's Arc*.

"Child, he's one of them club kids," Dash whispered.

Dash wasn't judging, *but he was judging*. Still I knew he was fond of Chaz because Dash would've kept his distance if he didn't like him.

The music in the club blared. It was a mix of techno and new trance music. It became evident that the clubs in WeHo refused to play hip-hop or R&B music unless there was a DJ club mix version of the song. On occasion, if lucky, they played Rihanna, Beyoncé or Chris Brown remixes, on Sundays—the *Black night*.

We practically had to shout to hear one another over the music. Chaz eased into the conversation the names of his celebrity clients, most of whom were 80s singers who hadn't had a hit song in years, and couldn't afford to pay for the services he rendered anyway because they were down and out.

Dash and I concluded that Chaz had a tendency to stretch the truth a bit. Not about anything serious, but about the money he earned doing hair and make-up. Initially, Chaz told us that he owned the salon, but he was renting a booth. He was even telling people that he was still collecting royalty checks from his small role on *Noah's Arc*. Nevertheless, we overlooked his tales because they were harmless—his intentions were good.

Dash's birthday fell on a Saturday, so he made plans to spend that weekend in Vegas, and Chaz jumped on board to help celebrate with him. I was unable to go because I was still calling home for money just to get by, but I offered to let them use my car to save on gas on the two hour drive to Las Vegas, since they both owned SUVs.

"I can't afford to go, but you can take my car. I can just switch with one of you," I said.

"Ok, I'll leave my keys for you," Chaz said.

Chaz and Dash left for Vegas that Friday and returned the following Sunday. I met them at the salon because I had laundry to wash—Chaz and I used the washer and dryer in the salon when the owner wasn't there.

Dash came into the salon briefly, but he was short on words. He said he was tired from the trip and left shortly thereafter. I called and texted Dash several times the following week, but I never heard back from him again.

6 CONNECTING DOTS

Dating was placed on the back burner when I lived in L.A. because I was afraid to trust my relationship choices. I couldn't seem to strike a balance between normal relationship imperfections and dysfunctional imperfections in relationships. But, living in L.A. offered the kind of isolation I needed for introspection. I've always known what I bring to the table of a relationship, but I lost sight of it after over-compromising a time or two. I discovered that I was confusing compromising with settling.

For me, dating was complicated in my 20s because I over-thought and overanalyzed things, and at times I was too unforgiving. I left no room for error. I held the men I dated to an unrealistic standard of perfection, which made it impossible for them to make simple mistakes. But the reality was that I was searching for their flaws as an excuse to walk away because at my core I was still uncertain whether it was wrong to be gay.

I should have taken the time to deal with the psychology behind the feelings that come with being gay before acting on them. I was ready for sex, but I wasn't prepared for intimacy—as in the case with Farrell, the first guy I dated. He had dated men before, even lived with a few of them, so he was sure of what he wanted and who he was. I caused much of the discord between us because I waffled on being gay and remaining closeted.

I concluded that I was once the broken, confused man who got emotionally tangled with gay men, who were ready for love, only to leave them holding their heart in their hands because I wasn't ready to live my truth. Consequently, I encountered the same kind of men I once was, because karma is patient.

Reflecting on the men I dated in my 30s allowed me to see that I had become too forgiving. Because I understood the journey to self-acceptance, unknowingly I suffered from the hero syndrome, which led me to try and save the men I dated from their brokenness. This was true in the case of Raylon, and a few of the younger men with whom I was involved.

Typically, I gravitated to men who were green about gay life because I figured they weren't emotionally calloused from heartbreak and disappointment, and I could shield them from the perils of the community. But, I've learned that I can't resolve anyone's issues or save them from the lessons life has for them to learn.

Subsequently, I made the decision to remain single for at least two years after Jacob. Nevertheless, I was invited out often. On one of my outings, I was introduced to Kina, a former member of the 90s R&B group Brownstone, and the voice behind the song *Girl from the Gutter.* We met at a one-woman show that was staged in Hollywood at a small black box theater on Cahuenga

Boulevard. After the show, I was re-introduced to Dorian, a girl I first met when I was in L.A. for the DIVAS Simply Singing AIDS benefit concert two years before.

After the play, a small group of us made our way across the street to Kitchen 24 for dinner and drinks. I was introduced to and unexpectedly fell in love with jalapeño margaritas. The bartender muddled the jalapeño before shaking it with the other ingredients. There was a spicy kick at the end of every sip. Hands down it was the best margarita I had ever had.

The eight of us sat in a front corner window booth talking over one another about the one-woman production, and life in general. Kina and I excused ourselves from the table to visit the dessert counter situated next to the host's stand to preview the petit fours. We made small talk at the counter, but I was careful not to mention that I was a writer because in L.A. everyone is somehow involved in the industry, and I didn't want to be another cliché. Kina also steered clear of any mention of her solo singing career, and didn't mention that she was once a member of Brownstone. There was a familiar energy between us, but I couldn't quite find the thread that would tie us together. Still, I knew we would become friends.

Several weeks later, I was invited to a barbeque in Silver Lake. Kina and Dorian were there when I arrived, along with a backyard full of other people—some of whom I recognized from television or film.

Kina and Dorian were the only people I knew, other than the host, so I stood close to them most of the day.

"Where do you live?" Dorian asked.

"In the jungle," I said.

"The jungle?! Oh my. Why there?"

"I know, right?" I said.

"It's not that bad," Kina laughed.

"Child please, it ain't that good either," Dorian said smiling.

"I just moved out here. I'm staying with a friend for now," I said.

Chaz wasn't really a friend though he had stepped up like a friend would, but I wasn't about to go into the entire story of how I ended up there.

"How do you like it over there?" Dorian asked.

"I don't," I interjected.

Dorian went on to say that she loved L.A. after moving from St. Louis four years earlier to work in the medical field.

Sunset was Kina's signal to head home because she had been at the barbeque most of the afternoon.

"I think I'm about to leave. I'm tired and I've been here for a while," she said.

"Ok, girl." Dorian hugged Kina goodbye.

"It was good seeing you again," I told her as we hugged.

"You too. Take my number. You have your phone?" Kina asked.

"Yeah, what's your number?"

I locked Kina's number in as she said her goodbyes and made her way past the fence on the side of the house.

"So, where do you live, Dorian?" I asked.

"I have a house in Pasadena," she said.

CRAIG STEWART

"Ok, I haven't been out that way yet," I said.

"If you wanna come stay with me, you're more than welcome. I would love the company," she offered.

"Are you serious?" I asked in disbelief.

"Yea, I have a three bedroom house. One of the bedrooms isn't finished, but the room you would sleep in is. At least you would have your own bed, and I'm hardly there. By the time I run my errands after work and maybe go to the gym I don't usually get in until about 9 o'clock at night," she said.

"Let me think about it," I smiled.

The offer was definitely appealing, but I didn't want to jump the gun and take a chance that things might not work out at Dorian's. I didn't want to burn a bridge with Chaz by moving out prematurely only to have to ask to come back.

"Ok, just think about it. I'm actually going home to St. Louis for the 4th, so if you want, you can housesit for me, and that way you can see how you like it. At least you'll have a weekend away to yourself," she said.

"Ok, I can do that," I replied.

"Ok, let me give you my number," she said.

Thirty minutes after Kina left the barbeque she called my cell phone.

"Hey. What you doing? You still at the barbeque?" she asked.

"Yea, I was about to leave though. I'm walking out now."

"Oh, ok. I got all the way home and didn't wanna stay in. I wanna do something. I wanna go somewhere," she said.

"Yea, I didn't really wanna go in yet either," I said.

78

"Where can we go?" she asked.

"You know I don't know," I said laughing. "But, I wouldn't mind doing something," I added.

Frankly, I was always open to going out in order to prolong going home to Chaz's place. But whatever Kina and I decided to do needed to be something relatively inexpensive or free because I had little to no discretionary money.

"I'm thinking somewhere in Hollywood. We can find a place to have a drink," she said.

"Ok, that's cool, but where?" I asked.

"Uhm…meet me at the W Hotel in Hollywood. You know where that is?" she asked.

"No, but I'll look it up on my phone," I said.

"It's right on Hollywood Boulevard."

"Ok, I'll see you in a minute. I'll call you when I park," I said.

"Ok."

Once we both found parking we made our way down Hollywood Boulevard to the rooftop bar of the W Hotel, which was swarming with people of every color and ethnicity—one of the things I loved most about L.A. There were people surrounding a fire pit and standing along the safety railings overlooking the skyline. The weather was beautiful with a slight breeze blowing through the night air.

"You want a drink? I'll treat," she said.

"No, I'm good, but thank you. So, Dorian offered me a room in her house."

"Really? That's cool. So, what you think? Are you gonna stay with her?" Kina asked, sipping her martini.

"I don't know. I don't wanna get over there and she has a change of heart. Do you think I should do it?" I asked.

"Yea, you should do it. She's cool. I don't think she would do that since she offered," she said. "Child, everybody loves them some Craig. A couple of the guys asked me about you. Everybody just wanna be around you," she continued.

"You stupid," I laughed.

"I'ma start calling you Belle! 'Cause you the belle of the ball, honey," she laughed.

"Ha! That's funny."

"I'm serious! I know my friends! I just watch them when they're around you, and I just laugh. I know them soooo well," she smiled.

Kina ordered a martini and together we people-watched, and talked until the wee hours of the morning about where we had been in our careers and how far we still wanted to go.

*****

Chaz was spending more time away from home once I was there to play care provider for his mother. I overheard his mother on the phone, leaving message after message, asking him to return her call for one reason or another, but he rarely called back. This was also true whenever Chaz and I were out together. Most times he looked at his phone, but ignored the call once he saw that it was his mother calling him.

I sent Chaz a text message to let him know that I would be house sitting for Dorian, so I would be gone for the 4th of July weekend. After I sent the text, I packed a small bag and headed to Pasadena. Before Dorian took her flight home to St. Louis for the Independence holiday, she texted me the code to get in through the garage door, as well as the code for the home alarm.

Once I was inside of the house, I took a seat on the couch to catch my breath and surveyed the house. It was peaceful. The house was quiet and there was no neighbor noise. I reached for my cell phone to send Dorian a message.

"I'm staying! LOL, I'm going to get the rest of my shit. See you when you get back,' I wrote.

"LMAO! Ok!" she replied.

"Thank you!" I texted.

"You're welcome," she replied.

The next day, I drove back to Chaz's, and packed the rest of my clothes to leave for good. Naturally, he wasn't home when I got there, so I sent him a text.

"Hey, a girl I know offered me a place to stay. She has a spare bedroom in her house, so I'm gonna move in with her. I'll still get the groceries for your place next month too. Thank you again for letting me stay. I really appreciate you," I wrote.

Thanks to my cousin Tiffany, I found many things to be grateful for while living at Chaz's, and I believe it's the reason God answered my prayers with a more comfortable living space at Dorian's. I lived with Chaz for approximately twenty-six days, and was moving to my third address in a matter of three months.

Chaz never replied to the text I sent him, but once I was settled in at Dorian's I sent him a thank you card and wrote a message inside.

When my food stamps for July became available, I went to Sam's Club to make good on the promise I made of buying groceries for Chaz's place. When I got to his apartment Chaz's Mom was happy to see me.

"Where you been?" she beamed.

"I moved to Pasadena. How you been?" I smiled

"I hate it here. I fucking hate this place. I wanna go. I fucking hate this place. I hate it. Damn, I hate this place," she said.

"Why? What happened?" I asked while putting away the groceries.

Chaz had asked me before not to put away the groceries for his mom because he said she needed to do some things for herself, and also if she put them away she would know where everything was placed.

"I never liked it here. It's hot. God is hot. It's so fucking hot in here," she said.

I stopped what I was doing to face her. I wanted her to know that I was listening and that she had my full attention.

"Have you told Chaz that you want to move?" I asked.

"Yeah, he knows. He knows. Yeah, he knows," she said.

"You should tell him again—that you want to live someplace else," I said.

She sat at the threshold of the kitchen and living room with her head hanging. She was wearing the same nightgown she had on when I last saw her. It was the first time I felt sorry for her. I couldn't think of anything else to say, so I showed her where I was putting the groceries and I left.

Chaz finally responded to my text message when he received the thank you card I sent him through the mail.

"You sent a thank you card to thank me? Did I send you a thank you card when I told you could stay with me?" he wrote.

"Chaz I thanked you consistently when I was there. How many times did I tell you how grateful I was that you opened your place to me when 'a friend' didn't? I sent a thank you card to show you that I appreciate what you did—that's called etiquette. And, I kept my word and bought groceries for your place even after I left. I didn't have to do that. I'm not there anymore. You're acting like I was paying rent and stiffed you," I replied.

"I'm just messing with you LOL. It's cool," he typed.

Behind every joke is a bit of truth, so I knew that Chaz wasn't joking. I ran into one of Chaz's friends in WeHo several weeks later who told me that Chaz was angry with me for many reasons.

First, I was no longer living at Chaz's place to play babysitter and care provider for his mom, while he ran the streets. Second, Chaz had a secret crush on me. In hindsight, his mood swings made sense—they only surfaced when he knew someone else was interested in me.

I made a few attempts to reach out to Chaz to stay in touch, but he didn't seem too interested in a friendship, so I stopped trying.

7 RESTORATION

Kina and I saw each other just about every day once I moved to Pasadena because we were now living within fifteen minutes of each other. Either Kina was visiting me at Dorian's, or I spent the day at Kina's, and at times I slept over on her air mattress.

We talked every day, all day, and she felt safe enough to share personal stories with me from her Brownstone days, which she rarely spoke about with others. Kina was even more open about her days as a solo artist. I could see a light in her eyes whenever she reminisced about an endorsement she had with Iceberg, the Italian luxury designer. She also beamed when she talked about being signed to the Wilhelmina modeling agency, and sold out shows under Benny Medina's management. But, as bright as the light was in her eyes, it quickly dimmed when she described when and why she walked away from it all.

Kina and I were becoming fast friends, and couldn't seem to get enough of each other's company. If we weren't jogging the Rose Bowl in Pasadena or the reservoir in Silver Lake, we were at

Venice Beach, or venturing to Harvelle's in Santa Monica for live soul music. In fact, any club with live music was our playground. Kina and I clicked as fast as Kepri and I had as undergrads at Hampton University, except Kina and I bonded over music.

"I looked you up," Kina said.

"Huh? What do you mean?" I asked.

"I googled you," she said.

"Really? What came up?" I asked laughing.

"I saw the stuff about your play—the stuff you said you did in Atlanta. It was all there," she said.

"I didn't make it up," I smiled.

I understood why Kina googled me. It was the very reason I didn't make it a habit of telling anyone in L.A. that I was a writer. I figured most people would question my veracity if it didn't appear that I was pursuing my craft actively. Nevertheless, I wasn't offended that Kina did some research on me since we were closer.

She too felt overwhelmed in ways by her career, and it was the familiar energy I felt between us when we met initially at Kitchen 24. There were many professional parallels that bonded us—things no one in our respective circles could understand. But, there were also similarities in our relationships with our fathers.

I had shared with Kina that my relationship with my father first became strained after he remarried and allowed his wife to overlook me every Christmas. I explained that my father's ex-wife bought a number of Christmas gifts for my dad, her adult children and their spouses, as well as my paternal grandparents, while I sat watching without a single present. My dad never said a word. Thus this habit continued every year that they were married.

"You still haven't forgiven your father. You're still that hurt little boy," Kina said.

"Why do you say that?" I asked.

"Because…you're different with him," she said.

"What do you mean?" I quizzed.

"You just are…there's a difference when you speak to your father," she continued.

"In what way?" I asked.

"Ok…when you talk to your mother on the phone…you come alive! You tell her everything you're doing. I mean everything! You go on and on, and the inflections in your voice change—just excited!" she said.

"Really?" I said partially shocked.

"Yes! But, when you talk to your dad it's like this, 'mmm hmm. Yeah. Ok,' …one word answers and you're off the phone in a couple minutes. You're…still…that hurt little boy! You gotta forgive him baby Craig. You gotta let that go," she said mocking me.

"I've never thought about it that way…That's true…You're right," I said.

I was still punishing my father for choosing his ex-wife over me—for making her his number one priority, and allowing her to mistreat me. It was the reason I closed him out of all the important details of my life, including my sexuality.

Jacob always believed I was afraid to tell my father that I was gay, but the truth was that I didn't believe he earned the privilege of knowing, so I closed him out.

It was time to finally have the conversation with my father.

*****

Kina wanted to build a one-woman show around some of the personal experiences she had as a little girl that followed her throughout her music career, and she enlisted me to help her.

"The reason I looked you up is because I've always wanted to do a one-woman show about my life. I've never found anyone that I could trust to share all of my stuff with, but there's something about you, and I can tell you're hungry," she explained.

I was ready.

"Let's do it! We just need to start meeting so we can outline the show."

"Wait, wait a minute. Let me finish," she laughed. "See, this is what I mean! You ready! You're like a little kid. You get so excited! I love it! I'mma start calling you Baby Craig—that's your new name. With that baby face and them dimples," she giggled.

"You crazy," I laughed.

"Seriously, you make me want it again, but I need to work at my pace. I can't feel rushed. I wanna ease back in slowly," she explained.

"Good! You should want it again," I said.

"I was so young when I got my deal. All of a sudden I had staff and payroll. I didn't know what I was doing, but I'm ready now," she said.

Kina and I had a similar relationship with music. We both had walked away from the business, but still craved the music. The difference between us was that she tasted success in a way I hadn't—her music had been released commercially. I had never placed a song on an artist's album, but Kina had toured with Barry White, singing background. Later, she joined Brownstone when they were the number two R&B group in the country, but above all she had released a self-entitled CD on the DreamWorks label.

"I just need to reach out to some producers to get some tracks so we can start writing. I've been out of the loop for so long," she said.

"I'm out of the loop too, but I can reach out to a producer that I know in Atlanta. I might be able to get us some tracks," I said.

"I'm excited! Baby Craig! You done brought the sunshine to L.A.," she beamed.

"You crazy. I'm excited too. I'm curious to see what we come up with," I laughed.

At our first writing session, we began framing ideas for Kina's one-woman show. We used Kina's laptop to organize storylines from the seminal moments in her life. We used the laptop to audio record her words as she spoke extemporaneously. Later we plotted where music would appear in the show's timeline.

I was exhausted after each session, and it was apparent that Kina was drained from releasing memories that she had stashed away to be forgotten.

After we'd been working together for a while, Kina made a confession. "There's something really special about you. I don't share like this in front of people, especially when it comes to my personal life and music ideas. And I was nervous at first about working with you, but you made it easy."

"Well good. That's what's up," I smiled.

"My friends are always asking to hear what I'm working on, and I could be working on something, but I would never say. I'm so private when it comes to my music when it's unfinished 'cause it's just an idea," she said.

"Mmmhmm," I understood.

"And, I used to feel like I had to explain what I was working on—" she said.

"Because you didn't want people to think you had given up," I cut in.

"Yes! That's so true! Oh my God. I'd be telling people, 'Oh, I had a meeting the other day,'" she laughed.

"Right! I know what you mean. But, I've decided I'm not making up stories anymore. I'll just say, 'It's coming in God's time.'"

"Mmmhmm. Yup…It's interesting because you said that you prayed before you moved to L.A., and before we met I was chanting for a writing partner. Then you showed up," she continued.

Kina practiced Buddhism and I was privileged on a number of occasions to witness her chant.

"Yup. So, while I was praying, you were chanting and the universe responded by connecting us," I smiled.

"Mmmhmm... You have this energy that makes people wanna to be around you. You've been like a breath of fresh air for me. I mean, being around you inspires me to work on something—write a song or practice the piano—because you want it so bad. I mean, it's all over you, and it's gonna happen... You're a writer—a for real writer. That's your gift. There's no doubt in my mind that you're gonna make it. It's just a matter of time," she said.

Kina was sitting directly across from me at her dinette. The smile on my face dissolved with embarrassment, then humility. She looked directly at me with her arms folded in her lap. I looked down at the laptop in front of me. I was flattered that she could see things that I was now struggling to believe about myself because of the many professional obstacles I had encountered. I desperately held on to hope, but was almost convinced it would never happen for me.

I had never considered a plan B per se, until life *happened* and seemed to disrupt things I had planned for my life. I seemed to be veering off course and the distractions caused me to think it would never happen. Over the years, I found myself working jobs I would never have previously considered, but dire financial circumstances warranted taking them. But Kina made me feel confident again.

"I'm telling you, you got it. I've seen what it looks like. I've been there. I've been to the top, and you've got it. Don't doubt that. It's gonna happen for you," she said adamantly.

My nervous smile became tears. I covered my face with both hands because I was embarrassed to be crying in front of her, yet I was so moved. I left Atlanta shattered by my relationship with Jacob and questioning if writing was my gift—if in fact it was what I was supposed to be doing with my life.

The tears were also brought on by the turbulent three months I endured being in L.A. Kina was confirmation. God was using her to speak to me. Our conversation and work together were the reasons I moved to L.A.—to reignite my confidence.

"Thank you…I appreciate you saying that," I said.

"You're welcome, but you don't have to thank me," she said.

"I needed to hear it. I've had so many setbacks."

"You're a writer, baby. You got it," she smiled.

"I didn't think I had it in me anymore. Felt like I was running out of time to do everything I wanna do."

"Unh onh, your confidence just had to catch up with your talent. That's all. One day we'll look back and say, 'remember how we used to dream about traveling the world?'" she said laughing.

"Ok! I know that's right. Let me wipe my face. You got me crying and shit."

"That's ok. You needed to get that out," she said.

After several days and hours of recording footage for Kina's one-woman show, we began concentrating on writing original music.

"I think we should just start writing and recording a bunch of songs and build a catalog and start licensing songs for TV and movies. We can make a great living licensing music," she said.

"I don't know how to license music," I said.

"I know how to do it. I've done it before. Mara, the creator of *Girlfriends,* licensed my songs before," she said.

"Ok, let's do it then. We just gotta get some tracks to write to, and a studio to record in," I said.

"I think I have some tracks around here somewhere," she said.

Kina dug up some tracks that she had tucked away until we got more from a music producer I knew in Atlanta. The first track we listened to we both loved. We put the song on repeat. Kina began humming a melody right away.

"That's pretty. Keep doing that. I like that," I said.

"I don't know what I just did. Melodies just come to me. I can come up with a melody like that," she said snapping her finger.

"Just keep humming. I'll record you with my phone," I said. I grabbed my cell phone and Kina continued humming melodies as they came to her.

It was a beautiful track, a mixture of hopefulness and despair. I began scribbling lyrics on a notepad. *This song was about Jacob and me.* It was an ode to how conflicted we both were about leaving or staying in our relationship.

I titled the song *Maybe Leaving is the Best Thing*, and thought back to what happened between us as Kina continued humming melodies in the background. The memories became the lyrics for the song.

"We started off as best friends," I wrote to Kina's melody.

I flashed back to every vacation, concert or event that Jacob and I attended. The first time I ran into Raylon, after vandalizing his car two years prior, I was with Jacob. Raylon was someone who pursued me vigorously. He had even moved from Tennessee to Atlanta with hopes of being in a relationship with me. But when I rebuffed his advances, he burglarized my apartment. He stole all of my winter clothes in the middle of one of the coldest months in Atlanta. I filed several police reports, but they did nothing, so I retaliated.

Jacob and I were going to a party when I spotted Raylon's car in the parking deck as we looked for parking. Raylon's car had been completely repaired of the damage I caused, but it must have cost his insurance company a small fortune. I reminded Jacob, before we went inside the party, what happened between Raylon and me because I realized in that moment that I wasn't completely over the anger. I was unsure if I would react once I saw Raylon face to face, but after I saw him the anxiety faded.

Of course, Raylon tried desperately to get me to look his way, but I saw him before he noticed me. Jacob and I laughed at how foolish he looked, but never acknowledged him. Raylon cackled and spoke extra loud the entire night, but I never made eye contact with him.

Kina continued riffing as I drafted more lyrics for the first verse and hook. I noticed Kina moving about the apartment; cleaning up dishes from the food we had earlier, but still humming.

"Oh, how everything changed, nothing is the same," I wrote.

"Forcing empty conversation," Kina sang.

"Yes, that's it!" I shouted.

"But so much more to say," I jotted down.

My mind skipped to the first in a series of arguments with Jacob that occurred as we were leaving a *Dining Out* magazine event at the Loews hotel in Midtown Atlanta.

On the drive home Jacob and I got into an argument that resulted in him telling me to get out of his car. Since I was only parked a few blocks away, I obliged and got out. He trailed as I walked to my car—begging me to get back in. But I refused so he sped off.

When I pulled into the parking deck of my apartment, Jacob was waiting in his car because he didn't have a key to my place. I had learned my lesson from Raylon, who used the key I gave him to rob me. Jacob followed me quietly into my apartment and began packing all of his belongings—things he kept at my place in the event he spent a night. He left without a word.

A few moments later, I heard his suitcase rolling in the corridor. The sound of the castors rolling on the floor got louder. He was coming back to the apartment. There was a knock on the door. When I opened the door, Jacob stood there with a smirk on his face—the same smirk he was wearing when I first asked him out.

He apologized and said that he didn't want us to fight. I warned that he might not be so lucky to come back in the future if he pulled another power move like the ones he had pulled that day.

I continued scribbling lyrics and thinking, recalling all of these events.

"We fight about everything and nothing at all. Maybe leaving is the best thing. Let me let go. So tired of being wrong cause you wanna be right. Maybe leaving is the best thing…" I sang.

"—to give up this fight!" Kina sang.

"Yes!" I said.

"Baby Craig, this song is a hit!" Kina shouted.

"It is! I love this track!" I shouted back.

"This a Mary J. Blige song. I can hear Mary on this," she added.

"Oh my God, yes! I can hear her singing this or Syleena Johnson. Ledisi would kill this!" I said.

"Yeah, Ledisi too. But, I don't know. I like this. I might want this for my record. It just depends on what my other songs sound like, 'cause I definitely wanna do more R&B. I wanna do soul music," she said.

"We need to record this," I said.

"I gotta get in touch with Camara—this is his track," she said.

"When was the last time you spoke to him?"

"It's been awhile, but I can email him. Hopefully he'll respond," she said.

Despite our best efforts to create magic a second time, Kina and I only managed to co-write one song together, because my time was divided once I secured a job with a commuter train company in Southern California.

Because we anticipated a change in our schedules we tossed around the idea of renting an apartment together in downtown L.A. or North Hollywood to write whenever the mood hit us, but we decided against the plan.

Instead, I moved into a place of my own with my first paycheck. I moved out of Dorian's and rented a room in a beautiful five-bedroom home in Westchester between Ladera Heights and the Fox Hills Mall. I was finally feeling settled in L.A.

8 LONELY IN L.A.

When I first moved to California, Dru told me that I would eventually feel lonely because she started feeling lonely around the six-month mark and that was typical for most people who moved to L.A. She asked me to tell her when I started to feel it, and sure enough, after eight months I was ready to leave California.

Fortunately, I had only signed a six-month lease because one year in L.A. was more than enough time for me to know that I didn't want to live so far from my friends and family long-term. L.A. taught me that fast friendships end quickly. I was cycling through people as quickly as I met them. I still hadn't heard from Dash three months later and my friendship with Dru was slowly disconnecting because our friendship had unraveled.

Mutual friends of Dash and mine revealed that his reason for withdrawing had nothing to do with me, but everything to do with his own depression. He was suffering silently because of his discontent with his personal life and the direction of his career.

And, once I moved to the Westside, I didn't see much of Kina except on an occasional Skype call.

I was beginning to see just how easy it was to feel lonely living in L.A. if you weren't a native. I spent much of my time hiking at Runyon Canyon, getting acupuncture, going to The Conga Room, or eating at some of my favorite restaurants like The Serving Spoon for breakfast, and Dulan's or Simply Wholesome for lunch and dinner.

Dating felt like a chore in L.A. because it seemed like most of the gay men that I was interested in were closeted out of fear that being openly gay would negatively impact their prospective careers.

I began dating an aspiring actor and model that I met at C Frenz, a gay club in Reseda. Noble appeared to be about my age, six feet tall or so and a solid 180 pounds. The night I met him, it was obvious that he was in shape because his plaid button-down shirt was open—revealing his chiseled dark brown skin. The tank top he wore underneath his shirt was damp from dancing. He was with a handful of guys, one of whom he was dancing with when I first noticed him. I couldn't tell if they were a couple or if they were just friends, so I watched for clues.

"I wanna wish a very happy birthday to Noble who's celebrating with us tonight!" the DJ yelled over the microphone.

Noble pushed his hand in the air and continued dancing as his friends surrounded him. I gathered that he was single when he switched to a new dance partner. I wasn't interested in a dance, but I was interested in knowing more about him. *Where was he from? Where did he live in L.A.?* But, the only way to find out was to approach him. Marcel, my former songwriting partner, taught me when I first came out that the dating pool is already shallow when it comes to quality, so I had to be brave enough to approach the men I was interested in otherwise I would be left with those who approach me.

As Noble and his friends were passing me to head out onto the patio in the back of the club, I tapped him on the shoulder. "Happy Birthday Noble."

"Thank you. How you know my name?" he asked suspiciously.

"The DJ just said it," I smiled.

"Oh, right," he said.

"Can I get you a drink for your birthday or is that your boyfriend?" I asked.

He looked around.

"Who?"

"The guy you were dancing with," I said.

"Oh, nah. That's my friend," he said.

"So, can I get you a drink?"

"Yea, that's cool," he said.

I could smell a hint of cigarette smoke on him, but I overlooked it as we made our way over to the bar.

"What you having?" I asked.

"Let me get a vodka cranberry," he said to the bartender. "So, what's your name man?" he asked.

"I'm Craig. Are you from here?" I asked.

"Nah, I'm from Shreveport, but I grew up in the Bay Area," he confessed.

At first glance, Noble was a regular guy, but his diction wasn't at all what I expected. He was very proper.

"Let me program your number in my phone man. What's your number?" he asked.

I've had the same cell phone number since 1999, and I didn't feel the need to change it because I was living in L.A.

"404...," I said.

Noble paused and looked at me after I gave him the area code. I thought about a conversation I had with someone in L.A. who said, "Atlanta is where the kids go to die," after I told him I had moved to L.A. *from* Atlanta. I was both shocked and uncomfortable by his candor. Perhaps, Noble had similar feelings about guys who lived in Atlanta.

"Ok. I'll hit you up. Let me catch up with my friends," he said.

"Ok. Good meeting you," I said.

I didn't bother asking Noble for his number because I figured if he was interested he would contact me. A few minutes later, Noble texted me.

"Hey man. It's Noble," he wrote.

"I got you," I replied.

"Cool," he wrote.

I finished my drink and headed back over the hill for home.

The next night, I received a text from Noble. He was on his way home from celebrating his birthday with a different group of friends.

"Yo, what you doing?" he wrote.

"Nothing much. At the house. What you up to?" I replied.

"Driving home. Just had a few drinks. Still celebrating my birthday," he wrote.

"Nice. Be careful…Where do you live anyway?" I wrote.

"Inglewood—off Florence. I'm horny man. You should come through," he wrote.

Before I responded, Noble sent me a naked picture of himself, and I was definitely enticed since I was in the middle of a sexual drought.

As I suspected, his body was lean and symmetric. He was careful to crop his head out of the photo, but his torso, dick and thighs were featured prominently. His dick was flaccid in the picture, but it was thick. I wanted to see a picture of his ass and didn't waste time asking for one, but he said that he didn't have a picture.

"If I come through I'ma need to slide my dick in you," I typed.

"That's cool. I'm not a pro at it. It's been a minute, but it's good mos def, LOL," he wrote.

"Is it smooth or hairy?" I wrote.

"It's a little hairy. I haven't shaved," he replied.

"I like it smooth. You mind shaving for me?" I typed.

"I can do that. Give me about 45 minutes to get ready," he wrote.

"Aight. Send me your address. Text me when you're ready," I typed.

Noble texted me his address and I put it in the GPS on my cell phone. He was less than ten minutes from where I lived. It was odd that we lived so close to one another, but met 45 minutes away in the Valley.

I showered, then slipped on a pair of jeans, a t-shirt and sneakers. Noble hadn't texted back and an hour had passed.

"You still want me to come? I'm getting sleepy," I typed.

"Yea, I'm shaving now. Leave out in fifteen minutes," he wrote.

"Ok," I replied.

I waited like he asked, then headed out.

Noble told me to park on the street and come through the side gate. He was renting a guesthouse that was nestled behind the main residence.

It was pitch black out. I could barely see where I was going. I couldn't see my hand in front of my face walking up the driveway to the rear of the house.

After I knocked on the door, he yelled for me to come in. Noble's place was quaint. It was all one room, and it was furnished with a couch on the right side of the room, a bed on the left wall and his closet was the back wall adjacent to his bed. Noble stepped out of the bathroom, which was just past the couch.

"What's up man?" he said.

He was completely naked. I got hard thinking about fucking him.

"Hey, what's up," I said.

"I'm tryna shave. I cut myself with these damn clippers, but I think I got most of it," he said.

"Don't worry about it. You're good," I said.

"Let me jump in the shower real quick. You can have a seat," he said.

"Ok," I said.

Noble walked out of the bathroom drying off with a towel. I had no idea his ass was so plump because it was hidden so well in his jeans. I watched his ass as he walked around the room folding clothes he had left scattered around his place. He sat naked on the side of the bed putting lotion on his body.

"Get comfortable," he said with a half smile on his face.

I stripped down to my boxer briefs, walked over and stood in front of him.

Noble pulled my dick out of my underwear and started sucking on it ravenously. He ran his hands along my thighs.

"You have a nice body man," he said looking up at me.

I grabbed his head and directed him. I pulled my dick out of his mouth and patted it on his lips, then circled them. He chased it with his tongue, bobbing and weaving his head, trying to predict my next move.

I leaned down and slipped my tongue in his mouth and sucked on his lips.

"Mmmm. Damn," he mumbled.

"Gimme that tongue," I whispered.

Noble stuck his tongue in my mouth. I pushed him back on the bed, and he wrapped his legs around my waist and pulled me closer. I kissed his neck and squeezed his ass with both hands. I lifted his ass slightly and slowly penetrated him. I felt his body flinch when I entered him—I grinded slowly. Digging deep inside him.

"Wait," he said.

"What's wrong?" I asked.

Noble pushed me back and swept his hand along my dick.

"What?" I asked.

"Is there something on it?" he asked.

"No, it's clean. There's nothing on it," I said.

"Let's just jack off," he whispered.

I lay beside him and held him. Noble wrapped my arm around him and held my hand in his palm. He curled his body like a spoon, and snuggled under me. I rested my chin on his shoulder.

We lay talking about our upbringings, how we both ended up in California, and about our dreams. Turns out Noble had lived in Atlanta briefly. He said that he almost didn't take my phone number because he didn't trust guys from Atlanta after being held against his will by some guys he met.

"I wish we had walked instead of running," he said.

"What do you mean?" I asked.

"I wish we had waited. You seem cool," he said before singing along to the music.

Noble's playlist consisted of a variety of Brazilian artists singing in Portuguese. He was teaching himself how to speak the language.

"You too," I said.

"Your voice is nice. I could listen to you talk all night. Has anyone ever told you that?"

Interestingly enough, I had always hated my voice growing up. I was mistaken for a girl over the phone quite a bit because the texture of my voice was thin, and I convinced myself that my voice was the indication that I was gay. In reality, my voice was typical of most pre-pubescent boys, but my insecurities sponsored a different story that led me to believe otherwise.

"I get that a lot now. The crazy thing is, I used to hate my voice as a kid," I said.

"Why?" he asked.

"People used to mistake me as a girl, especially at the drive thru window," I said.

Noble burst out laughing.

"Ma'am is that all? Can I get you anything else?" I recalled.

Noble laughed harder. He laughed until his stomach hurt.

"Really? Is that what you gon do?" I said jokingly.

"Yo...I'm sorry man. That was funny as shit though. My bad," he said still laughing.

"It's alright," I laughed.

I could see a lot of myself in Noble. He was *me* when I was with Carrington. The tables had completely shifted. He had aspirations of becoming a working actor, but the auditions were few and far between, which meant money was very tight for him because the gigs that he landed were even more spread out.

Since I was working fulltime and Noble was having financial difficulties, which meant whenever we did things together, I paid. I tried to ease his worries by sharing my hardships with him. I knew the lessons that I had learned weren't just for me, but for him and for whomever else I chose to share them with.

More importantly, I tried to be proactive in the way I supported him. I offered to buy some groceries for Noble because I knew his pride wouldn't allow him to ask me for help. But, Noble's financial frustrations weren't our only obstacle. He was conflicted about his sexuality. His biggest internal battle was whether or not he *wanted* to be gay, and his career was his main excuse for hiding. He told me that he would only date men for a period in his life; that one day he would marry a woman and have a family. Noble sounded a lot like my friend Brent who had broken away from the Hettabrinks for the same reasons.

There comes a point in every *relationship* when we have to know when to push and when to pull—whether or not we should walk away or try harder. The moment that Noble confessed that he intended to have a wife someday was the moment I knew I had to let go of the idea that we would be more than friends, if anything at all.

Every person who comes into our life has purpose whether it's a brief encounter or a long-term relationship. Lessons in consideration are sometimes as subtle as someone holding a door open for us. Noble taught me that I had developed a pattern, at some point along the way, of dating men who were severely closeted. Unconsciously, I gravitated to men like Noble who weren't interested in building a relationship because it offered me protection. It was a defense mechanism for me to avoid heartbreak again.

There was a part of me that *knew* these men weren't looking for anything long-term, so in that regard it was *safe* for me because there would never be a break up to brace myself for or to grieve because a relationship wasn't on the horizon—it wasn't a part our discussions. There were never conversations about being in a relationship because that wasn't the end goal for either of us.

This particular pattern also fed my ego because it meant that I could pass for straight in public if these men were willing to chance being seen out with me. It proved to me that I could move through the world without sounding the alarm on my sexuality or theirs. I believe many gay men—on some level—want to know that they can navigate the world without being spotted.

The beauty of patterns, however, is that we can break those patterns once we're honest with ourselves about them. My experience with Noble taught me that I never have to compromise the joy of being myself for the sake of being with someone—ever.

9 A *PEACE* OF MIND

I returned to Atlanta almost one year to the day after I left for Los Angeles. I missed the life I had in Atlanta, and I also missed my friends. In the short year that I was away so much had changed. The city was different, and it wasn't just because of the new construction sprouting up on just about every street corner in town. It *felt* different because I was different. I had a renewed sense of self; therefore, my perspective had changed.

It was refreshing to again be surrounded by so many young professionals and entrepreneurs making their way, and not just talking about the things they wanted to accomplish, like in L.A.—a city full of dreamers, the land of pretend, where everyone has something to prove and desires of becoming somebody. I was reminded why I had fallen in love with Atlanta when I moved there in 1998. Atlanta was the place where young entrepreneurs moved because the city celebrates artists and entrepreneurs for their accomplishments—whatever they are—without them being a major success first.

Nevertheless, L.A. had restored me in a sense. My experiences in California taught me that I had accomplished a great deal in my life, but hadn't given myself enough credit for those things because I didn't have the material possessions or financial stability as proof of what I had done. I realized through the stories I heard from some of the aspiring writers, dancers, actors and singers that I met in L.A. that I had done much of what they were dreaming of someday doing. I had already begun sharing my work, my gift, with the world.

I was glad to be back in Atlanta for a better quality of life too. It's a city where one can live well with little. It was easy to acquire a beautiful apartment with modern appliances, sometimes stainless steel, with granite counter tops, for $900 a month or less.

On the contrary, that same $900 in California *might* get you a single dwelling in the Valley with old carpet, no appliances, and no amenities. In L.A. proper that money would afford you a room in someone's house, maybe a private bathroom, with all of the utilities included.

I missed the ease of getting together with friends, and in Atlanta spontaneity was easy for meeting up to get a drink or a bite to eat someplace—that sort of spur-of-the-moment meeting was difficult to duplicate in L.A. Part of the difficulty in L.A. is that most people have multiple hustles, which prevent them from being available at a moment's notice, and the lay of the land is just too spread out for impromptu meetings.

The biggest question for me, on returning to Atlanta, was whether or not I was really in control of the sexual temptations that lured me before. Would I be triggered merely because I was back in Atlanta where the options for sex are plentiful—not because it's Atlanta, but rather, because there's an influx of gay men?

I had encountered a series of broken men in Atlanta before I moved away, which was part of my reason for leaving, but their brokenness wasn't concomitant of Atlanta. There's this idea that dating or love is harder in Atlanta than in any other city. I don't believe Atlanta is the problem. I believe it's a corrupted mindset of many gay men, in cities that are heavily populated with other gay men. With that, some of the men in those cities refuse to take themselves off the dating market completely to focus on a single partner, even after they meet someone.

The aura of brokenness is present in any city around the world where gay men are persecuted and feel shame for being gay. Part of the pain and disappointment that we experience as gay men is tethered to the relationships we have with our family, and the other portion is tied to how we treat each other in our community, and on the dating scene—which usually links back to Internet hook up sites and mobile apps.

Returning to Atlanta forced me to wonder if there were triggers that I may have been unaware of that would draw me back to casual *and* anonymous sex, or if the impetus for my behavior was a byproduct of a past depression. I recognized similar self-destructive behavior on the gay mobile apps as I did with the online sites that I used to patrol. There was a sense of detachment present on the sites, and a level of toxicity that I knew all too well from wading through those poisoned waters previously. Thus, I could never pretend *not* to know what I knew to be true from experience with the sites.

Most of us frequent these sites and phone apps under the guise of entertainment or fun, but in actuality we're looking for acceptance or too ashamed to admit we're looking for companionship. Oftentimes, we walk away from the apps feeling worse than before we logged in, especially if our messages are ignored, or when someone becomes inconsistent after a few messages back and forth. In return, we respond to someone else with hurt because we feel rejected or frustrated.

I understand that the men I meet online could potentially be the same men that I meet in public, but I know for certain that the Internet emboldens us to say and do things we wouldn't ordinarily do face to face. People don't generally present themselves in person in the way most do online. And, men who lurk online often set up even greater lines of defense and *generally* operate with little to no consistency or integrity. Most don't bring their best self to those sites. I could see the old me in some of the profiles that I read. I recognized the emptiness and loneliness right away.

Everyone online isn't there for casual sex, but the majority of the participants are, and I believe once the majority pollutes the water it tends to poison the mentality of all who drink from that well. It's the reason most profiles read, "This is just entertainment. I don't take this app seriously."

To that end, I knew that if I wanted a greater chance to build something significant with someone I would have to take an alternate route. I decided not to partake in the sex sites or the mobile apps because love is elusive there. I had learned the lessons from being online, and didn't need to shift a former *addiction* to another medium. This time around I was looking for more than entertainment and casual sex.

After perusing a gay chat forum to ensure sex wasn't the priority on the site, I created a profile. I used the medium as a means to chat and was open to the possibility of dating since I was approaching the two-year mark of being single.

I came across a page that was *clean*. It wasn't dripping with references to sex and the profile didn't have any naked pictures plastered on the page, so I sent a message.

"How u feeling man?" I typed.

Almost immediately I received a response.

"Hello, I'm feeling very well, man, and thank you for asking. How are things with you?" he typed.

"Things are great, man. My day has been productive. I'm getting some work done now. I'm Craig. Your name?" I wrote.

"Hello Craig. I'm Rocky and nice to meet you," he replied.

"Nice to meet you as well," I typed.

I was working on plans to re-launch my greeting card business, Say it in a Card.com. I had been planning for weeks to host a rooftop party for my 36th birthday and for the re-launch, and the re-launch was approaching in three days. The weather forecast predicted thunderstorms, so I was busy searching for a new venue to redirect the guests I invited.

A few minutes passed and I got an alert that there was a new message in my inbox from Rocky.

"So Craig, your ad doesn't say much about who you are other than your stats. Tell me about the real you. Why are you here on this site?" he wrote.

"I've been single over 2 years, ready to settle down now. I'm from Maryland, but I just moved back to Atlanta from L.A. Yourself?" I wrote back.

"I'm on here because I enjoy the photos of nice looking men and occasionally what they say in their profiles. Sometimes it makes me disgusted, sometimes it makes me laugh, and sometimes I'm intrigued. I've met a few quality men on here, but it's been few and far between. My bar is set very high, so I may interact with someone on here, but never plan to meet. I don't believe everyone I chat with on here is meeting material, nor do I believe that every time I meet someone on here that I have to engage in sex. Don't get me wrong, I have had many horny days and nights, but I'm not a fan of having sex with random people. I have had a few one nighters though. I'm human, but I definitely know when I've found what I like," he typed.

Rocky unlocked more of the pictures on his profile for me to see. There were several pictures of him in various locations. Some were casual pictures of him in Miami and on vacation in Dubai swimming with dolphins.

"*smiling* You're handsome. You opened your pictures without me asking, and I appreciate the integrity in your answer. I agree wholeheartedly. I've had some one nighters too, but it's been years. Where are you from?" I typed.

"Thank you for the compliment ☺. You're handsome as well and I'm not just saying that because one compliment deserves another, LOL...I'm from Charlotte, North Carolina, but I'm in Dubai as we speak...well, as we type," he wrote.

"What do you do?" I wrote.

"I work for the US government—NOT MILITARY...I'm writing a book that's loosely based on my life. I don't believe everyone's story is book worthy, but I truly believe mine is. I've had many experiences, met many interesting people and I've been to almost every part of the world. There is so much inside of me that I have to get out like my 10-year relationship with a man, who was my first, his 5 kids that I raised, and now juggling a marriage with my past...It's just so much....LOL. I can't say much of course because I'm still in the process of writing ☺," he typed.

"Wow, that is a lot to put in a book. Good luck writing your book, and kudos to you for the 10-year relationship...How long are will you be in Dubai? Do you live in Atl? And what time is it there, LOL?" I typed.

"I plan to stop doing so much traveling for work at the end of the year or in the spring of next year. I do enjoy seeing the world though and being able to share my experiences with family and friends...I do not live in ATL, and it is 7:46 p.m. here," he wrote.

I looked up at the clock on the stove. It was 11:46 a.m. He was eight hours ahead. I was a bit disappointed when he told me that he wasn't in Atlanta, and overseas for another eight months, I knew there was a strong possibility we would never meet and it was pointless investing too much energy or time. Nevertheless, I continued messaging.

"That's great…I see your picture in Dubai with the dolphins. I've always wanted to do that. I have a couple friends that visited Dubai. I've never been, but I've traveled a bit in my day," I wrote.

"I swam with the dolphins at Atlantis in Dubai and I was a little afraid at first," he typed.

"Nice…Well, I'm glad you were in the Atlanta chat, else I wouldn't have seen your page. So, what are you using this site for? Just to see the photos or otherwise as well?" I wrote.

"I guess I'm open to the possibilities of friendship, and if that friendship blossoms, then...well you know ☺," he replied.

"LOL, yea, I know. I feel you. I think the best relationships spawn from friendship. The past 2 years being single has allowed me to put that into practice and break old patterns," I wrote.

"You seem like a great guy and I hope we can continue this conversation, but of course not on here…I'm going to grab dinner, and then shower to wash this gym sweat off my body. I'm salty right now…LOL. Not sure if the time is right to exchange phone numbers, but I do like to keep in contact with family, friends, and associates via Skype if you have it," he wrote.

Rocky included his Skype name and email address with the previous message.

"I do have Skype. I'll send the request. You're not ready to call me internationally yet, LOL," I typed.

"LOL," he replied.

Initially, I couldn't find Rocky on Skype, so I asked him to add me instead. But, as soon as I asked him to add me I found his Skype ID and sent the request.

"You found me after all," he messaged on the Skype instant messenger.

Before I could respond to his message, my computer was ringing. Rocky was calling me on Skype. The computer rang three times before I answered. I wasn't certain that I was going to pick up. It may have been dinnertime where he was, but it was still morning for me. I hadn't put my contacts in, so I was still wearing my glasses, hadn't brushed my hair or teeth, nor had I washed my face, but I picked up anyway.

"Hello," I said smiling.

"Hey there. I had to say hello live before I step out for dinner since you added me," he said with a grin on his face.

He was more handsome on camera than in his pictures. The picture was fuzzy then clear and fuzzy again because the Internet connection on the military base where he lived wasn't the best.

Rocky and I talked for four hours like long lost friends. Our conversation was so fluid that he never left his room to have dinner in the dining hall. Instead, he ate tuna and crackers to curb his hunger, and we video chatted until he started falling asleep. And even then, neither of us wanted to end the conversation.

10 SMITTEN

Rocky was the first thing I thought about the next morning when I woke up. I should've been finalizing plans for my birthday and the re-launch party, but I was daydreaming. I thought about how serendipitous it was to meet him online in an Atlanta chat room considering he was in the Middle East. But more important, I thought about how easy it was for our conversation to flow without any mention of sex.

There was something very different about Rocky—I could tell right away. The only misfortune was that we weren't in the same city to develop it, and I didn't believe in beginning a relationship long distance, especially with someone I had never met in person. In a sense, Rocky was evidence that there were like-minded men out there interested in the kind of relationship I wanted. The challenge was finding someone in the same city or at least the same country whose relationship values were aligned with mine.

In the past, I tried to *train* the men I dated how to be in relationship with me, but we found ourselves in a constant tug of war. We pulled each other in opposite directions because our views and values on relationships were different, so essentially every argument was about the parameters, and which way to move the relationship.

I picked up my cell phone to check my text messages and emails. I noticed an email from Rocky.

"You popped out of nowhere and made my day...........SHAME ON YOU!!!!!.........LOL," he wrote.

Obviously, he woke up with me on his mind too. He had sent the email from work, and from the time stamped at the top he had sent it as soon as he got in the office.

*"*smiling hard* I say as much...,"* I replied.

"I really enjoyed our conversation and we should definitely talk often. I guess I like you a little bit, LOL," he wrote.

"I can make that happen ☺," I replied.

We agreed that we wouldn't use Facebook to learn about each other. Instead, we would let things unfold naturally between us, but I couldn't resist. I was curious to know more. I used Rocky's email address to find him on Facebook. I really just wanted to see more of his personality, which I could have gotten from looking through his pictures and posts.

Rocky's profile picture was one I had seen on his profile from the chat site we met on. The next picture that I saw was of him in a limousine—another photo that I recognized from his profile on the chat site. The third picture I saw was his Facebook cover photo, and it was a photo of a wedding party. He was standing with a bride. *He's married?* Rocky was pictured with his wife, and an elaborate wedding party on their wedding day.

I signed into my chat account to message Rocky. When I signed in, I noticed that Rocky was already signed in online.

"Hey you. Where were you in that picture that you have up with the tuxedo on?" I messaged.

I didn't ask Rocky directly why he hadn't told me that he was married because I was curious to see if he would be forthcoming.

"In a limo," he replied.

"I know, but where were you going?" I typed.

"To my wedding," he replied.

"You're married??" I typed.

"Yes, I told you that yesterday," he typed.

I rifled through the message thread that we had exchanged the day before and realized that he had told me he was married in the second message that he sent to me. *How did I overlook that?*

I guess I was so enraptured by his first gay relationship that lasted ten-years that I completely overlooked the message about him being married. *So, why was he married to a woman now?*

"Wow, I missed that," I replied.

"We got married last year in June, but I've been thinking I made the wrong choice by getting married. When I see myself in a long-term relationship I see myself with a man," he wrote.

At the time, Rocky had only been married for eleven months, and most of that time he and his wife were living apart in separate countries.

"Why did you get married?" I typed.

"It's hard to explain, but after I broke up with my ex-lover I knew that he and I weren't getting back together because I was no longer attracted to him, and we were growing apart. So, I accepted the job over here, and I met my wife soon after. Plus, you know how it can be with guys. I was tired of the games they played," he wrote.

"It's not like that with every guy. I don't play games, and I don't think it has to be that way," I replied.

"I'm not saying all guys are like that, but that's what frustrated me. And, before I met her, I prayed that if God sent me a woman who could accept my past and love me, for me, that I would take it as a sign to get married," he messaged.

"But you had been with a man for ten years. Perhaps, you misread His message. What if God was trying to show you, through her, that your attraction for men was stronger?" I wrote.

Rocky explained that he met his wife in Afghanistan when they were both on assignment there—she as a high-ranking officer in the military and he as a contractor on the military base. He said they were engaged for four years, and that he dated guys during the course of their engagement.

One of the longest relationships that Rocky had while he was engaged was with a guy he met and worked with in the Middle East. Rocky said they were together for two of the four years that he was engaged to his wife to be. Before returning to the states permanently, the man tried to persuade Rocky to call the wedding off. He told Rocky that over time he would be unable to get aroused for his wife, but Rocky ignored his advice. Rocky thought he would still be able to perform sexually once they were married because he had sex with an ex-girlfriend when he was in high school. But, it had been more than a decade since Rocky had been with a woman.

Rocky confessed that he only broke off the relationship with this particular guy because it became violent. Rocky learned that his boyfriend was seeing another man on the base, so he confronted him. Naturally, his boyfriend lied, so in retaliation, Rocky slept with the guy that his boyfriend cheated with, which led to the altercation.

Once the dust settled, Rocky continued to have sex with his ex-lover, though he maintained that he would never be in a relationship with someone who became violent. When I asked why he continued sleeping with him after their fight, he didn't have an answer.

Oftentimes, in gay relationships, physical abuse is *discounted* because it's reduced to a lesser offense. For some reason, pushing, shoving or punching doesn't qualify as abuse because it's not deemed battering because we're all men. But abuse is abuse and there's nothing normal about that at all.

Seemingly, we've become *functionally* dysfunctional. Relationship dysfunctions appear to be more attractive than normalcy in many relationships, straight or gay, because some have become so accustomed to dysfunction that without drama they don't know how to operate.

I asked Rocky about his wife's knowledge of his past. *"Does she know that you had a ten year relationship with a guy before you moved overseas?"* I wrote.

"No. She just knows that I've been with a man before. She doesn't know details," he replied.

I didn't understand how he could omit the fact that he'd been involved with someone for a decade.

"That's significantly different. You had a life with him. I bet that would've made a difference. Does your family know that you're gay?" I wrote.

"My family knows. I came out to them when I was eighteen. I sat them all down in the living room one day and told them," he wrote.

I was intrigued and more curious with each email sent. *"How did they take it?"* I wrote.

"My mother didn't like it at all. Her hair fell out from the stress," he wrote.

"So, no one said anything when you told them you were getting married?" I typed.

"No, my family wouldn't do that. They know how I am. They wouldn't dare do something like that," he wrote.

"I guess they were happy you were 'no longer gay,'" I wrote.

"But they never had to deal with it. I was in the army for about six months. I was stationed in Louisiana. My ten-year relationship was in Baton Rouge away from my family," he explained.

"How did you get out of the military?" I typed.

"I told them I was gay, but they didn't believe me. My ex said he wasn't gonna wait for me to do a six month tour in Kuwait. So, I called my mother 'cause she didn't want me to go to Kuwait anyway, and she told them that I had told the family I was gay when I was eighteen, which I had. And, they discharged me," he wrote.

"Then I really don't understand you getting married," I wrote.

"I know the day will come that I will leave this marriage. I just haven't met anyone that's given me a reason to do it now. It's not urgent," he wrote.

I just couldn't let that go.

"But leaving shouldn't be contingent on meeting someone, but because you're gay and that's your truth. That's more than enough reason," I typed.

Rocky's one-year wedding anniversary would fall one month after he and I met online. He told me that he and his wife were meeting in Thailand to celebrate. She would be flying from their home in Tallahassee and he would of course leave from Dubai.

"I'm planning talk to her in Thailand anyway because we're not as close as we should be. I wanna see where her head is. She may be feeling the same way I am. I know she loves me, but she may not be in love with me. That connection just isn't there like it should be," he typed.

My suspicions grew when Rocky told me that he and his wife communicated sporadically. He said they could go a couple of weeks at a time without talking on the phone, especially if he didn't reach out to her first. When they did talk, their calls were always brief because they ran out of things to say. Rocky was a classic example of a gay man that could potentially be an incredible partner; yet, he was locked away in a marriage to a woman playing charades. Nevertheless, Rocky and I continued to speak every day, on an average of three hours a day on Skype. We also communicated throughout the day offline, either by text or email.

Because of the eight-hour time difference we never experienced a lapse in communication. When Rocky's day was beginning in the office, mine was coming to an end, leaving us time to email back and forth until I fell asleep. And, as I woke, he was finishing his day and heading back to his room for the night, which left us time to talk for hours at a time on Skype. The only interruption was the poor Internet connection on the military base that sometimes forced us to end our calls when we lost the connection.

But, without fail, there was an email from Rocky every morning when I woke up.

"Good morning," he wrote.

"Good morning. You're beginning. I'm ending," I typed.

"Let's begin and end, together............ ☺," he replied

"Be careful with your words. I take words seriously. Well, actions, too ☺," I wrote.

"I do choose my words carefully, Mr. Stewart and you should take them seriously ☺," he wrote.

"Mr. Stewart, LOL. That was funny," I replied.

"You were on my mind heavily................SMH. I absolutely cannot believe this at all. I can't tell you this enough, but every time we communicate, it brings me so much joy and I never want the conversation to end. Your voice is so enduring to me. I could listen to it forever......LOL," he typed.

"☺ I enjoy talking to you too. It's nice to know we're on the same page," I answered.

"I really like you, man."

"I like u more…So, you getting a divorce?" I asked.

"Yep," he wrote.

"You're gonna have to 'cause I ain't no side piece LOL," I wrote.

"I don't expect you to be."

"I'll allow fate to have its way," I wrote.

"One day at a time," he replied.

"What are you gonna do with me?" I asked.

"Fate, remember?" he wrote.

"Yes, but fate meets destiny at the intersection of choice. We have choice in every matter. Happiness doesn't just happen. It's a series of good decisions."

"I'd figure it out," he wrote.

"How's your day going so far? I'm up looking at YouTube. Just ate a bowl of cereal. I'm a night owl," I replied.

"My day is going great. Today was really warm and my body has been clammy all day long. I'm looking forward to taking a hot shower when I get off, and snuggling up under my covers

with the air turned up. After that, I look forward to seeing your face, even if only for a few minutes," he answered.

"Ok, I'll message you when I get up to see where you are so we can Skype. Enjoy your day. Be safe," I wrote.

"Ok, have a good night. Sweet dreams, handsome," he replied.

Before I drifted off to sleep I decided to check my email once again, and there was another email from Rocky.

Craig,

I went to the gym and just got in from lunch. Right now, I'm just sitting here at my desk. I should be working on something, but I'm in deep thought. You always leave me pondering on something. I'm intrigued in a mighty great way. Did I also mention that you inspire me? Really, you do. Thank you. P.S. I think I'll take your phone number now LOL.

Rocky

I replied to Rocky's email with my cell phone number. Fortunately, we both had iPhones, so our text messages were free as well as our phone calls, Since the landlines on the military installation were statewide phone numbers.

The seeds were planted, but only time would tell what would happen, if anything at all.

11 FORBIDDEN FRUIT

On the morning of my birthday, I woke up to a Happy Birthday text message from Rocky. He also asked me to text him the name and address of the venue for the re-launch party because he wanted to invite two of his friends to support my greeting card business. Rocky kept in touch with many of his gay friends even after he was married. In fact, one of his groomsmen was a friend from his *former* life.

I decided to have the event at 10th & Piedmont, a restaurant and bar that occupied the former location of OutWrite Bookstore in Midtown Atlanta. Rocky called me for the address after I neglected to send it to him via text.

"Hey, don't forget to text me the address. I need to send it to my friends, so they can come by to support you," he said.

"Oh, my bad. I forgot to send it. I'll text it now," I said.

"Are you at the place yet?" he asked.

"No, I'm about to leave now to set up. It's pouring down outside," I said.

"Ok, well good luck today. Send the text," he said.

"Thanks. Ok," I said.

Shortly after I arrived at 10ᵗʰ & Piedmont there was a floral delivery. The delivery woman struggled to open the door and carry the arrangement.

I was excited.

"Those are for me!"

"Is there a Craig Stewart here?" she asked.

"Yes, that's me," I smiled.

My mom was known for sending me surprise birthday and Valentine's Day gifts, so I assumed the dozen yellow roses were from her. I pulled the card from the arrangement, *"I hope these bring a little sunshine to your day. Happy Birthday. Your special friend, Rocky."*

I couldn't help smiling. Some of the guests asked who they were from, but I refused to say. I had received flowers before, but I was flattered by the gesture more because he was out of the country and made time to locate a florist to send them.

"I just got the flowers. Thank you! So, that's why you really wanted the address, LOL," I texted.

"Yeah, LOL. I was trying to make sure they could deliver them before you got there, but my friends are coming too, so look for them," he texted.

"You get major points for this, thank you," I texted.

Immediately he answered.

"Good! I like extra points. When you get a chance text me a picture of them, so I can see them," he texted.

"Ok. And I'll text you when I leave here."

"Ok, I may be sleep. I'm gonna try to go to bed early tonight, but try anyway," he replied.

Before I had a chance to contact him, Rocky sent me a text message late in the evening.

"I just got back to my room from the chapel. I have so much on my mind. I was praying about all of this, and started crying. I was crying so much that I have a headache...I've never met anyone like you. I don't think I've ever felt like this about anyone. I don't even know if I felt like this with my ex-lover of ten years...I wish I had met you before I got married because I would never have gotten married...I'm about to go to bed, so you don't have to reply. I'll talk to you tomorrow."

"Why you crying, babe? It's ok...You had to get married. Otherwise you would've always wondered, what if? Get some sleep. We'll talk tomorrow," I replied.

Rocky and I spent more time communicating than some couples who live in the same house, and I didn't take that lightly. We were learning each other's idiosyncrasies through our conversations on Skype, but we were very much in sync. He often texted at the exact moment that I was thinking about him, or in the process of texting him, and the same was true for him.

I took a few chances calling him at work outside of his normal work schedule, and ironically, he would just so happen to be in the office because he forgot something there, or he was working late. But, either way, he was there to answer the phone with, "I was just thinking about you."

Before long we could read each other's body language. I knew when he had something heavy on his mind because his eye contact on Skype was scattered. At the same time, he could always tell when I was in my head about his marriage, or about our future together because I was short on words.

I told Rocky that I was planning to move back home to Maryland in the summer—after just nine months in Atlanta. I wasn't re-adjusting to the city in the ways I expected. And I wanted to spend time with my family after the re-launch of my greeting card business. Rocky's concern was where I planned to settle down if he and I were ever to be together because I didn't seem to be sure where I wanted to live.

We both wondered if the synergy between us on Skype would translate in person. The tricky thing about long distance relationships is there can be a false sense of connection because face-to-face time is limited. Thus, the tough conversations are often avoided because the time together is a commodity, and better spent enjoying each other—leaving the issues on the sidelines with the potential to compound later.

But, Rocky and I were masters at communicating. We left nothing to assumption. Even if it meant sending an email in the middle of the night to reassure the other that we were still on the same page, we did. We weren't afraid of looking too interested or trying too hard.

Once Rocky's one-year wedding anniversary was just days away, I grew increasingly anxious. Our Skype conversations became more about his marriage and the impending discussion with his wife. The anxiety between us snowballed, and it was evident on our Skype calls because I wasn't so sure that Rocky would go through with the conversation with his wife. Occasionally he made Facebook posts about how much he missed his wife, and how he couldn't wait to be home with her for good. But then he would email me when I became distant.

Craig,

I know you're probably asleep right now, but I just want you to know that this journey we are taking together is very exciting to me. I mean, getting to know you has been an easy thing to do. Discovering our differences, dislikes, and some of the things we agree to disagree on, has been interesting as well. Seeing how we resolve our issues has really been an eye opener for me. The way you try to understand me and encourage me makes me want you more. The things we have in common and the things we don't have in common make you the perfect match for me. I am so looking forward to seeing the other sides of you that I've yet to experience. Thank you for being patient with me. Thank you for trying to understand me. Thank you for just simply being YOU ☺.

Rocky

Rocky knew that he wasn't being fair to his wife, but he feared that the two of us wouldn't work. Whenever Rocky wanted to discuss something that involved his feelings, or something that was difficult for him to say he corresponded through text messages or emails, as opposed to just saying it. Thus, some of our Skype calls were part conversation and part instant message.

"I really do like you, but I'm also mindful that we still have not met or spent any time together," he wrote.

"I'm sure it will be the same in person. We wouldn't be able to talk for hours if we couldn't get along," I answered

"But, you could think I'm a jerk in person," he wrote.

"I think I would know that after a month of talking to you every day, all day," I said.

"I don't doubt that when we do meet, it'll be awesome, because you are an awesome person."

"Do you realize how long we always talk?" I wrote.

"Of course I realize it. I want to be a big piece of your life. I mean........that's what my gut tells me at this moment," he wrote.

"So, follow your gut...I want you to recall the moment, the exact moment, when you fall in love with me," I replied.

"Sometimes when I'm looking at you............there are no words to describe what I'm thinking or feeling—when I'm talking to you as well. Sometimes words aren't necessary. As much as we love them."

It was important to me that he know how I felt.

"I'm just trying to soak it all up. Stay present in it. I do think about when you come home—for good," I wrote.

"I know, right?" he said.

"Six months is a long fucking time to wait!" I burst out.

"It's long to you, but I'm used to it. It's really not that long. It's gonna fly by. It'll be here before we know it," Rocky answered.

I wanted to feel closer to him.

"Send me one of your t-shirts or something, so I'll have something of yours and I'll know what you smell like, LOL," I said.

"Ok, I'll send you one of my funky gym shirts," he laughed.

"I didn't say all that," I chuckled.

"I'll send you a t-shirt and this body spray I use before I go to the gym. It smells really good. Actually, I need to order some more 'cause I'm getting low. I'll order you some too. I think you'll like it. Send me your address," he said.

"I'll send you something too, but it's gonna be a surprise. Send me your address too," I smiled.

Rocky kept food and other snacks stashed away in his room for the nights that he missed the dining hall, as he did on the first night he called me on Skype. He also kept food for the days that he didn't have an appetite for whatever the dining hall was serving. So, I figured I would send him a care package with some of his favorite foods and snacks that he didn't have access to in the Middle East. And, I would also slip one of my *Say it in a Card* greeting cards in the box, too, for an extra touch.

"Hey, email me some music too. We get music late over here. Send me some current music that people are listening to now," he said.

"Ok, I'll email you a mix of my favorite songs," I answered.

"I believe we will learn much more about each other in Dubai or wherever we decide to meet for the first time," he typed staring at me.

"I would love to come there. I guess we would have to look at dates that work, and make plans for it to happen…That's a long ass flight to take alone," I wrote.

"I have a three week vacation coming up," he said.

"When is your vacation?" I quizzed.

"Sometime in October. I have three weeks off. The plan is to go home to Florida for a week, then visit my family in Charlotte for a week, then come to see you. Then we'll fly back to Dubai together for a week. I have to check with my boss about the exact dates," he said.

"I could stay in your room?" I asked.

"No, we would stay in a hotel," he laughed.

"Oh, I was gonna say," I laughed. "So, the first time I get some of that booty will be in Maryland," I laughed.

"Nah, you 'gon have to wait 'til we get to Dubai," he laughed.

"Shiiid, ain't no way in the world we're gonna sleep in the bed the entire weekend just to wait to get to Dubai! That would be hot though. But you ain't gonna be able to wait either," I laughed.

"Boy please. Watch and see."

"No, you watch and see. You ain't gotta give it to me 'cause I'll take it."

"You ain't taking shit," he laughed.

"Ok. You'll see," I said.

We made plans to meet in Maryland once Rocky was in the states.

"So, the first time we meet will be in Maryland—my stomping grounds," I said.

"Mmmhmm. I've never really been there. I've been *through* there, but never spent time there or D.C. really," he said.

"Ok, so, we'll stay in Baltimore for a night and in D.C. for the second night."

"Yeah, 'cause I wanna see the White House," he said.

"Mmmhmm, and the Washington Mall and the new Martin Luther King Memorial," I added.

"I'm gonna ask my co-worker for the name of this seafood restaurant there too," he said.

"Ok. How much are the plane tickets to Dubai normally?" I asked.

"Depends when you get them, but a cheap ticket is like $1,300. But, I'll pay for half of your ticket since the government pays for my tickets to fly home," he said.

"But how are we gonna split the cost of the ticket?" I asked.

"I'll just put half the money in your account, and you just buy the ticket. Just don't run off with my money," he warned with a chuckle.

"Please," I laughed. "Ok, well, you gotta let me know in advance so I'll have time to save the money for the flight," I said.

"I will. So, when you get a chance send me your account number and I'll wire half the money to your account and you can just buy the ticket," he said.

"Ok, I'll send it to you, but we need the dates first," I said.

"I CAN'T WAIT!!!!" he typed on Skype messenger.

"Me neither. Me. You. Dubai," I replied.

"I want to lick your lips," he wrote.

"You better know what you're doing with these lips," I wrote.

"Oh, I know what to do with them, LOL. I see your silver on your chin, LOL. CUTE!!!! I like that gray in your beard for some reason," he wrote.

"I'm not gray anywhere else, so enjoy it, LOL," I typed.

"I love you," he typed.

"I love you too," I replied.

12 BITTEN BY THE LOVE BUG

Rocky and I were both uneasy about not being able to talk during his anniversary vacation. His trip to Thailand was the first time that we would be separated by a day or two without contact because of the travel time between Dubai to Thailand. Not to mention, he would be with his wife, so there was a good chance that we might not be in contact at all for the entire week.

Rocky was also uneasy about the prospect of having the conversation with his wife about his sexuality, and his desire to leave their marriage. Still, I wasn't totally convinced that he would go through with the conversation in Thailand because he waivered often. He vacillated between telling his wife in Thailand, and telling her after he and I met to be sure that *leaving* was the right thing for him to do.

I've never been one to just exist in a relationship, so I didn't understand Rocky's way of doing things. As my friend Cris often said, *"I'd rather be alone feeling lonely than be with someone and feel like I'm by myself."* To me, it's better to be single if being in a relationship means *compromising the joy of being myself or sacrificing peace of mind.* And, a life of deception doesn't offer peace of mind.

The pieces of the puzzle were beginning to fit. Rocky learned, from a former co-worker that his wife was had fallen in love with a female officer when she was stationed overseas, which was more reason for him to have a heart-to-heart conversation with her. There was a great disconnect between them because he was gay and she was a lesbian.

"It sounds like you want to wait to see what she wants to do, and you'll follow suit. If she's gay, then she could very well be waiting for you to say something. What if she's just afraid to have the conversation too? Both of you could be afraid to broach the subject," I said.

"Craig, I know the outcome may be divorce, but we are talking about a marriage, not a boyfriend and girlfriend. It's going to be a task to put all that behind me. I just want to make sure that I'm in a clear headspace when and if it happens," he said.

"*May* be divorce? *If* it happens? One minute you're saying you are getting a divorce. Then you act like it's up in the air," I said.

"I may have worded it incorrectly. It's not based on what she wants to do. It will be based on us being honest with ourselves and each other," he explained.

"I'm beginning to think it was a mistake getting this close to you since you're not single. I think we should stop before I begin to resent you," I said.

"I still believe the time will come. It's not a question of *if* I'll tell her; it's more about *when* and *how* to tell her. I'm gonna do what I said I was gonna do, but I don't wanna be pressured. I need to do it in my time," he said.

"You're right. You do have to do it in your time, so we should step back so you can do that," I said.

"Stop talking crazy," he said.

"I'm not talking crazy. I'm being serious."

"It's a process Craig…One of the things that scares me is whether or not you'll be patient through the process. It's not gonna happen overnight. It could take a year to divorce," he said.

"I understand it's a process, but you have to begin putting things in motion. It may take a year to divorce, but it doesn't take a year to separate," I snapped.

"I feel like you're pressuring me. This is why I don't like to talk about this and I just keep it to myself," he said.

"I'm not pressuring you." I said.

"Well, why do you keep bringing it up? It seems like every time we talk now, we talk about this," he fussed.

"I'll tell you what, I won't mention it again," I said.

We sat silently as Rocky continued packing for his trip to Thailand. Suddenly he laughed.

"You make me sick."

"What?" I said trying not to smile.

"You know I can't stay mad at you."

"I'm not gonna avoid having the conversations we need to have for fear that you're gonna get upset either," I smiled.

140

"I know. I'm not saying that. I just don't wanna think about that right now," he sighed.

"All right, well, have a safe flight and I'll speak to you when you get back," I said.

"Unh onh! You know I can't go a week without talking to you. I'll talk to you while I'm gone!" he laughed.

"How do you figure?"

"They got Wi-Fi! If I have to leave the room to Skype you real quick I will...Or email you on Facebook," he laughed.

"Ok, I'll talk to you later. Have a safe flight. I love you."

"I love you too. Bye boy," he said.

Still, I prepared myself not to hear from Rocky for the five days that he would be on vacation with his wife.

A day and a half passed with no word from Rocky. Naturally, I wondered what he was doing and at what point he would have the conversation with his wife. I figured it would take a few days for him to build up the courage, but still I wondered.

Periodically, I checked his Facebook page for pictures to surface and eventually they did. Rocky looked happy in the pictures with his wife. Or at least he pretended to be, even if he wasn't. With each post, I was overcome with doubt, more questions and some jealousy.

The comments left under the pictures by his Facebook friends and siblings were baffling because theoretically his family knew he was gay. It was quite the contradiction, yet they were celebrating this sham of a marriage.

Rocky emailed me on Facebook soon after he uploaded the first photos to his page. I was rather short in my responses, and he picked up on it right away.

"Hey, I just wanted to send you a message to let you know that I made it to Thailand, and I've been thinking about you every day," he wrote.

"Hey, how are you?" I replied.

"I'm good. I'm having a lot of fun. There's so much to do," he wrote.

"Yeah, I saw your pictures," I wrote.

"I can tell you're upset. We'll talk when I get back to Dubai. I miss you," he answered.

"Ok, be safe."

That same day, Rocky called me on Skype from his laptop. He was standing outside of the hotel.

"Where are you?" I asked.

"I'm outside. I had to see your face for a minute. Make sure you're ok," he smiled.

"I'm good," I lied.

"No, you're not 'cause I wouldn't be, but ok," he smiled.

"You think you know me," I laughed.

"I do," he said.

"Where's your wife?" I asked smugly.

"She's in the hotel room. I told her I'd be right back," he said.

"Mmm," I muttered.

The video screen on Skype was blinked out and froze, and the sound was crackling off and on. The service in Thailand, at its best, was worse than the service in Dubai on a horrible day.

"This connection is really bad. Let me get back inside. I'll email you later," he said.

"Ok, I'll talk to you later."

"I love you," he said.

"Love you too," I answered.

I know that love offers no guarantees, but sometimes we expect some sort of contingency that every relationship is intended to be a forever kind of love—when in fact some relationships are designed to teach us how to let go. With that, I reminded myself that it was ok for me to date others because Rocky and I weren't exclusive. *He's married* and he may not leave his wife.

Once Rocky returned to Dubai, he confessed that he didn't have the conversation with his wife. He said there wasn't enough time for them to talk because they had plans every day that they were together. But I believe he got cold feet. He said that he would have the talk with her once he came home on his three-week vacation in October because there would be more time for them to discuss things.

In no uncertain terms, I told Rocky that it would be best if we took a few steps back so that he could decide what he wanted. I made a conscious decision to space out our communications, and became less available to him. I stopped answering every call that he made to me, and I was no longer in a rush to reply to his text messages.

Instinctively, Rocky felt the change immediately, and emailed me.

Craig,

I do appreciate your openness and honestly about how you feel as well as your expectations. I don't want you to stop communicating with me. It seems as though despite what you've said, you did still choose to withdraw yourself from me and I'm very sad about that. I'm hurt. I do understand that you are putting yourself in a precarious emotional space when dealing with me and that is why I try to handle you and our situation very carefully, because the very last thing I want to do is hurt you. I love you, man. I opened up to you because I wanted you to know where my head was as well as all the possibilities, good or bad. I hope you don't regret any connections or feelings we have for one another. You are far better than I am with words, so I would love to talk to you soon, if you are up for it. Again, I really love you and my connection with you...I wouldn't change it for the world. You are very special to me and don't ever forget or doubt that.

Rocky

My instincts alone were enough to let go because I had chosen not to allow insecurities or fear of being alone to lock me into another bad situation. But, I heard someone say once, "One of the hardest parts of life is deciding whether to walk away or try harder." I was torn. Part of me thought I should ignore Rocky's email, but a larger part of me wanted to respond, so I did.

Hey there,

Before you went to Thailand, you were adamant about having the conversation about where things are, and it didn't happen. I'm starting to think it will never be the time to talk when you come home because you don't wanna broach the subject. You were gung ho a couple weeks ago about speaking to her face-to-face when you learned that she was involved with a female officer, but my guess is when you get home you'll lose the zest to approach it again. Things will die down by then, and it'll no longer be an issue. You don't want to be the bad guy—the one at fault for ending the marriage. And, no matter how disconnected you are in the marriage you think it's better to coast along.

Craig

In the past, I often *gave up* on love before giving it a valiant try. The idea of trusting Rocky completely frightened me. But remember, *there are degrees of trust*. Trust isn't limited to the confidence that your partner will remain faithful, so I'm not just speaking about *trusting* that Rocky wouldn't cheat on me like he was cheating on his wife. Trust extends to judgment. A huge part of choosing a *compatible* partner is choosing someone whose *judgment* you trust. There's a level of trust that comes with giving someone your heart, but that's very different than trusting their ability to make great choices both inside your relationship and outside of it that will impact you both. There was no doubt—I was questioning Rocky's judgment. While I was debating our relationship, he sent me another email.

Babe,

I know you have some concerns in regards to my marriage. I have concerns as well. I wonder how my life would be. Would I date? What would the divorce process be like and what kind of toll would it take on me. It seems very draining every time I hear someone speak of a divorce. What if she gets pregnant? What if she wants to stay together despite everything? Would I still say, "It's over?"

Would I lose you as a friend, if I stayed with my wife? I really think if things don't work out with us, I'll lose contact with you, or we would only stay in touch because I make the effort. I also wonder how long it would take for me to figure out what I'm going to do? I have many, many thoughts about this on a day-to-day basis. I think about what it would be like spending the rest of my life with you. Would we be the happy successful couple setting the bar for how real love is or should be? Will we love each other enough to fight through it all? Will we WIN IN THE END?

Rocky

Rocky thought leaving his wife was a gamble because it was possible things might not work out with us. But in an email to him, I reinforced the idea that winning was the only option if he was doing it for himself.

Rocky,

Honestly, I thought a lot of things. I thought about dropping off for a while to self-protect and to give you time to think, and get clear about what you need and want. I thought about cutting off contact with you completely. I thought about asking you not to contact me until you've figured out what you're really going to do. No texts. No calls.
But, dropping off without communicating was a pattern I broke before I met you. I want to communicate my feelings and leave nothing to chance.

I thought more about the precarious emotional space I'm putting myself in because after the email you sent today you're still unsure what you're going to do. You're still thinking long term with her, but fantasizing about a life with me. You mentioned the possibility of her getting pregnant, but you can't perform sexually; and having a kid wouldn't turn things around for you.

I thought about the connections I could have made, but avoided because I felt it would fuck things up with us. And it seemed pointless to start something new with someone else only to break away when you come home. I wonder if that's been smart on my part, and if you would do the same for me if the tables were turned. I've been going along with some of this to prove to myself that I could be patient, but I'm cheating myself.

Craig

His response was almost immediate.

Babe,

I feel as though a part of you already belongs to me, and NO, I don't want anyone else to have it. It's unrealistic for me to ask you not to date, and as painful as it might be, not to have sex with someone else. I know that it's not your nature to have random sex with just anyone, but if you did I wouldn't have any grounds to stand on as far as being mad.

Rocky

Hey there,

I'm thinking about our last conversation. It's safe to say WE BOTH have unspoken expectations of each other. Although I never say, 'I want you to take the steps to get out of your marriage when you come home' and you never say, 'I don't want you to see anyone else. Wait for me to come home,' the expectations have been set and are there no matter how unrealistic they are.

Craig

The following morning when I woke up, I had several missed phone calls from Rocky's cell phone. I generally slept with the ringers turned off, so there was no way I would've known he was calling. There were two voice messages from Rocky.

"Babe, call me back. I have Delta on the line. I'm trying to book your flight for Dubai and I need your sky miles number," he said.

The next message was a part of a conversation he was having with the ticketing agent.

"No, that's not his birth date. I'm sure he was born in '76, not '75," Rocky said.

I tried calling Rocky back, but he didn't pick up. I looked at the times of his calls and an hour had already passed, so I sent him a text message.

"Hey babe, I was sleeping. Are you still on the phone with the airline?" I texted.

"You're late. I've already booked the flight. I needed your birth date. They had the wrong birth date on your sky miles account." he replied.

"So, you already booked the ticket?" I texted.

"Yeah, 'cause somebody had to make shit happen. You should have the itinerary in your email," he texted.

"LOL. I don't have the money for my half yet," I replied.

"Just put it in my account when you get it," he texted.

"Ok, LOL. Send me your account number when you can. I'll put the money in your account when I have it. I'll let you know when I'm putting it in your account," I texted.

"Ok. I gotta go. I'm in the yard. I'm not in the office. I'm not supposed to use my cell out here," he replied.

"Ok, text me when you get to your room,"

"Ok," he texted.

"I love you," I texted.

"Love you too," he replied.

I trusted that Rocky had strong feelings for me, but I didn't have complete trust. I was struggling to believe that he had the capacity to be faithful. I wondered if he was only cheating on his wife because she wasn't a man, or if he was a cheater because he was a cheater at his core.

13 HOMECOMING

I moved home to Maryland two weeks before my brother Jimmy was released from prison. Jimmy had served 23 years for the murder of his ex-girlfriend's ten-month-old baby girl—a crime that he still maintains he didn't commit. Jimmy was locked up in 1989, when I was still in middle school, but after I left home for college I didn't see him until his release in 2012.

Jimmy and I spoke occasionally over the phone whenever I was in Baltimore on a visit from school, and he happened to call home. But I hadn't seen him in person since I was 17 years old— eighteen years had passed.

The drive to see Jimmy on Maryland's Eastern shore was three hours in one direction, and the drive home from school in Hampton, Virginia was three and a half hours in a different direction, which made a trip to see him on a weekend visit almost impossible. And, as my mom got older she took the trip to see him less frequently.

I returned home to live for several reasons. For one, it made sense to be home with my family to cut down on overhead because the cost to print the greeting cards combined with my personal expenses were great. I didn't want to find myself in the same financial predicaments I had been in before I moved from Atlanta to L.A.

Secondly, I wanted to be closer to my great niece and nephews because they barely knew me. I had lived away from home since before they were born. I wanted to have a relationship with them, and quick turnaround visits home weren't enough to achieve that. Generally, it took them several days to warm up to me, and just as they got comfortable being around me it was time for me to leave again.

And, when Jimmy was released, I wanted to be there to help welcome him home, and assist him in making a smooth transition from prison to the real world.

Before Jimmy came home the family chipped in to buy him new clothes, shoes, sneakers, underclothes and suits to interview for a job. My sister Donnie took the liberty of getting him a cell phone and adding him to her cell phone plan.

My mom planned an elaborate dinner at the house for my immediate family. This included me, my nephews Ty and Terrell, my sister Donnie, and Kenyetta, Donnie and Jimmy's sister on their dad's side. We all planned to be together after we picked Jimmy up from prison. We had a separate dinner outing planned for the extended family the following Sunday.

My mom's menu was complete with fried fish, steamed shrimp, homemade Maryland crab cakes, fried chicken, and she enlisted my aunt Gloria to prepare seafood salad—a family favorite—macaroni and cheese, and tossed salad.

When he returned home, Jimmy had to learn a whole new skill set. He had no clue how to use a computer, send an email, or a text message. So I offered to send him to a computer class, but he never agreed to take the class. He opted instead to find a job right away because he was most interested in getting a car and a place of his own, instead of sleeping in my mother's basement.

Although we never believed that Jimmy committed the murder, for the first time in Jimmy's life, he said that he wanted to live on the right side of the law because he had sold drugs for most of his adult life. But transitioning back into the real world proved to be a challenge for him.

My brother secured a warehouse job four months after his release; nevertheless, things that are simple for most of us were frustrating for him, such as being in a crowd of people. He said he felt like he was experiencing a panic attack when we assembled our entire family at a restaurant the first weekend he was home. I imagine large crowds were reminiscent of prison fights he'd once been involved in or had witnessed over the course of his imprisonment.

Jimmy also had to adjust to the luxury of privacy. He was so used to bathing in a community shower that he had to break himself out of the habit of wearing his underwear in the shower, and bathing himself with them on. He said the first weekend that he came home—out of habit—he climbed into the bathtub still wearing his underwear.

And, as quick as Jimmy was paid from his job, he was broke. He wasn't used to having money, so he spent it on whatever he wanted the second he had some.

*****

I decided to tell my father that I was gay one evening when he stopped by my mom's house to see me. It was a secret I had shared with my mother when I was 23 years old, and over time shared with my maternal family.

I finally wanted to make peace with my father about all that had transpired between us while he was married to JoAnne. I felt that part of this healing process required me to unveil a part of my life that was closed off to him—my sexuality.

My mother and I were at home in the kitchen when my dad knocked on the front door. When she made her way upstairs to use the restroom, I ran upstairs after her and waited in my bedroom. I caught her going back down the staircase. My father was still sitting in the dining room.

"Ma," I whispered.

"What?" she asked.

"You think I should tell my father now?" I asked.

"Tell him what?" she quizzed.

"*That I'm gay*," I said frowning.

She paused for a moment like she had some things to consider. Over the years, my mom had asked me several times when I planned to tell my father that I was gay, and I sometimes joked that he would find out when he called my house, and my live-in partner answered the phone. Of course, my mom didn't think that was funny, and she didn't think that was the way he should find out. But she did agree that this was the right time.

"Yeah," she said.

Secretly, I was hoping she would agree because I wanted her to be there if my father had difficulty with my disclosure. I followed my mother back downstairs and took a seat at one of the barstools in the kitchen, and my mom sat in the dining room with my dad. I was facing my dad, and my mom was seated next to my dad, but with her back to me, so she was seated between us.

"Dad," I said. My heart pounded. I thought my voice would drop, so I took a deep breath.

"Yeah, Slim," he said looking directly at me.

I looked him directly in the eyes.

"There's something I wanna tell you."

"What is it?" he asked.

"I had a lot of time to think about things when I lived in L.A., and I realized that I was closing you out of significant details in my life and why," I said.

"Mmmhmm," he mumbled.

"I thought about how the divorce affected me—" I said.

"Craig, I told you then not to worry about all that stuff. That was between me and your mother," he interjected.

"Yes, I know, but it still shaped who I became. Even the things that happened between us with the child support and you not wanting to send it after you and JoAnne got married," I said looking directly at him.

My father exhaled heavily, but he listened closely to what I was saying.

"It's the reason I never invited you to Atlanta to see the play or any of the greeting card parties I had. And why I never shared anything personal with you. It's the reason I never discussed my sexuality…with you," I said.

Again, my father exhaled heavily, and for the first time during the conversation his eyes shifted. My father looked away. His eyes shifted down to the floor, then back at me.

"My mother already knows. I told her when I was 23. I just never felt like I could share that with you," I said.

"I didn't see this coming," he sighed.

"I knew when he was a little boy," my mother said casually with one elbow planted on the table and her head resting on the back of her hand.

"I didn't know. It's a surprise to me," he added.

"Well, you couldn't have been paying too much attention. Parents know if their children are gay or not. That is, if they're not in denial," she said.

We can remember a story any way that we choose, but the truth is *always* the truth. Obviously, my mom had a memory lapse concerning what happened when I first told her.

For a moment, my eyes connected with my dad's and the room was silent except the background chatter from the television.

"You're still my son. I'm gonna love you no matter what…I've always told you I'm proud of you, Craig. I'll always be proud of you…You're *my* son," he said.

"I love you too," I replied.

The fact is, my father digested the news about my sexuality better than my mom had twelve years earlier, but I didn't bother reminding her.

*****

I confided in my sister, Donnie, about Rocky being married, which proved to be a mistake for many reasons. If I wasn't torn emotionally before telling my sister, I was definitely torn after, and regretful that I had told her at all.

"So listen, I'm gonna tell you something, but don't go running your damn mouth," I said.

"Boy, what? I ain't gon tell nobody," she said.

"Rocky's married," I said.

"What?? Child, shut up! To a woman?" she asked.

"Yea," I said smugly.

"Well, isn't he gay?"

"Yea, he's gay," I said.

"Umph, umph, umph. Well, what he get married for?"

I shrugged.

"That's what I asked," I said.

"Well, when is he gonna tell her? 'Cause he needs to leave that marriage. That just don't make no sense," my sister said.

"He's supposed tell her when he comes home."

I had already told her about our plans to meet up later in the year.

"Shit, that's in October! He needs to call her and tell her now from right over there," she said bluntly.

"He doesn't wanna do it over the phone," I said.

"Why not? All he gotta say is, 'Look, I don't wanna be married no more.' Shit that's simple," she said.

"Would you want somebody to tell you that over the phone? Plus, he doesn't know what she might do with their house while he's overseas. He wants to be home just in case it gets ugly."

"And see, your ass is making excuses."

"No, I'm not!" I laughed.

"Yes the hell you are," she laughed.

"Donnie, you talking like you just walked away from your marriage. I recall having to push you 'cause you were making excuses too," I said.

"Yeah, but—"

"But nothing! With your judgmental ass!" I laughed.

"No, but look. When I did leave…," she continued.

I interrupted her.

"Mmmhmm, here she go."

"No, listen! When I left I said he can have all that shit! See, Rocky is full of shit! What she 'gon do to that house? Her ass ain't crazy. She gotta have somewhere to stay. Shit, that ain't nothing but a house. He can get another house," Donnie continued.

"But it still takes time to build up to that. You had many reasons to leave, but you were overlooking things, and even got into a knock-down, drag-out argument with me over the phone, then hung up when I told you to leave him! Then when you *finally* woke the hell up, you called me crying and apologizing for getting mad at me," I reminded.

"Yeah. True," she said.

"And Rocky is also worried about the money he's been saving," I added.

"Child please! Unh onh! Wait 'til his ass call here again on Skype. I'm sure gon' tell him," she said.

"You better not! Donnie, I'm telling you! You can't say nothing to him 'cause that's not your place to say anything!" I laughed.

"Why not?" she asked.

"Because! That's like if something happened in your relationship, and you confided in me, then I go back and pull up whoever you're in the relationship with *about something you told me*. That's not my place!" I said.

"Yeah, well, watch me! 'Cause his ass needs to either *shit* or *get off the pot*," she said walking away.

As promised, my sister confronted Rocky the first time he called me on Skype and she happened to be there.

"I didn't know you *was* married!" she said half jokingly and half seriously.

"Stop being so loud! Mommy's in the other room. You know she listening!" I snapped.

My mom had always given me good advice, but this wasn't something I was ready to share with her, so I didn't want her to know.

"Oh,…I didn't know you was married," Donnie said again, but this time she whispered.

"Mmmhmm," Rocky mumbled.

"Why did you get married?" she asked.

"Craig and I discussed this. He knows," Rocky said.

"You need to leave that marriage. When are you gonna get a divorce?" Donnie pressed.

"I'm gonna take care of it when I come home," he said.

"But, why did you get married in the first place if you knew you liked men?" she continued.

"Craig and I have already talked about this," he said.

"Ok, that's enough. Move!" I said turning the laptop away.

"Wait a minute—" Donnie said.

"No, 'cause you asking too many questions," I said.

"You a trip," Donnie laughed.

After she left, Rocky said he felt ambushed, and I understood why he felt that way. In the past, my sister would only appear on Skype with me to make general conversation with him, and she often complimented him for being handsome. This time, Rocky felt judged and had no qualms about telling me that I should've stepped in sooner to prevent the confrontation.

In a sense, he was right. I could've done a better job at shielding him because he was blindsided. But I knew Donnie had my best interests at heart and didn't want to see me get hurt in the aftermath of Rocky's indecision.

14 BUTTERFLIES

Love is for everyone, but relationships are for the emotionally mature because relationships don't heal insecurities, or cure emptiness and loneliness. I've always believed love was possible, but after several failed relationships. I was caught somewhere between being jaded and hopeful. It felt like all of the relationship stories that I heard were the same, just with different characters.

The issues that I've faced with dating men aren't unique, and I would *never* suggest that the men I dated were completely responsible for the demise of our relationship. I've become clearer about how my behavior or response to certain situations aggravated my relationships and contributed to the fall-out. After all, we've all been someone's disappointment.

But, I was burned out from trying to have relationships with men who were fundamentally different from me. I attracted guys who had very different core values than mine—men who wanted the kinds of relationships that didn't work for me. Thus, I made up excuses about why I shouldn't open up again.

With Rocky I believed love was possible again for me. Was I still nervous with him? Absolutely. Not just because he was married, but because he challenged every fear and every concern I had about love and relationships. Sure, I could've talked myself out of any involvement with him because he was married, but I listened to his experiences, some of which scared me, while others reminded me that I'm not close to perfect either, and never will be.

Soon after the conversation with Donnie, I heard from Rocky again.

"Can you login to Skype please?" he texted.

"Ok," I texted back.

I grabbed my laptop and signed into my Skype account. Rocky's profile was green because he was waiting for me online.

"Hey, what's up?" I said.

"Nothing. I was just laying here thinking," he said.

"What you thinking about?"

"Look at you! You can't wait! You just know it's about you," he laughed.

"No, I'm just listening," I laughed.

"I wanna tell you something, but I don't wanna talk about it. I just wanna say it," he said.

"Ok," I replied.

"I wanted to tell you that I think about you a lot—more than I think about my wife…I go through my day trying to figure out when I can fit in time to call you at some point during my day— before work, at work, before I hit the gym. And honestly, I don't even do that for my wife. I mean, since I met you I don't really think about her. I have to remind myself to call her...I care a lot about you...a whole lot. So, I just wanted to say that, and you don't have to say anything back," he added bashfully.

"Ok," I smiled. "That was hard for you to say huh?" I tried to hold back a laugh.

"Yeah, I don't usually say stuff like that," he smiled.

"I appreciate you saying it. It's nice to hear."

"I just hope you can be patient," Rocky added. "'cause I know if things don't work out exactly as you think they should, I'll always have to reach out to you to stay in touch 'cause I know you're not gonna stay in touch with me," he admitted.

"You said that before. Why do you say that?"

"I can just feel it," he said.

"You're probably right," I answered. "but this is a good test of my patience, so in a way it's teaching me patience. But, only time will tell. If you come home and start putting things in motion I'll wait...I know a divorce can take time, but I would need to see a separation or something. If you don't get the ball rolling, then I'm not waiting, 'cause I didn't sign up for this. I'm not putting my life on hold to wait for you to find the courage to leave your marriage," I said.

"Craig, we have property, insurance, and accounts together. It's not that simple," he said.

"I get that," I interjected.

"It's a process. It's gonna take time to separate that stuff."

"I understand that," I added.

"And I do care about her. I feel like you just want me to be heartless and not care about how she's gonna feel. I think about all sides of this every day," he said.

"I'm not saying you should be reckless. And, I'm not saying you should be heartless, but you do have to be responsible. The longer you wait the harder it will be. It's not gonna get any easier…Would you wait for me if the tables were turned?" I asked.

"I can't say what I would do because I'm not in that situation," he said.

"Of course you wouldn't," I said.

"But, again, I do think about things from your side too. I do. And, it's not fair," he said.

"All I'm saying is, I want us to go into this with some level of integrity, and that starts with you telling her before we start having sex. I don't want you to think in the back of your mind that I'm ok with this because I'm not. That's why I stay on you about it," I explained.

"I don't think that. I know you're not ok with it. If I don't know anything else, I know that," he said.

Rocky pleaded for me to believe that everything would work out the way we both wanted, so I gave him the benefit of doubt.

*****

Six months had passed, and it was time for Rocky to come to the states for his three-week vacation. It felt surreal. It was hard to believe that we were only days away from meeting in person. I thought back to when we met, and all that occurred up to this point including our ups and downs. I couldn't believe we had made it through six whole months together.

There is a middle ground between showing consistent interest in someone, and smothering him or her. I had experienced more than a handful of dating scenarios where there was a lack of consistency out of fear of looking *too* interested. Frankly, Rocky had been more consistent than anyone I had ever dated, and he was overseas. Never did I feel that he was afraid of showing how interested he was in me.

We both put forth the effort to maintain a connection until he came home. In addition to our daily communications, I received small, unexpected gifts from him in the mail so we could feel closer. For instance, there was the body spray that he sent me like the one he used before his workouts. And then there were the souvenirs he picked up for me when he was in Thailand—a Kingdom of Elephants t-shirt from Phuket Fantasea, a key chain, and a glass Classic Coke soda bottle.

In return, of course, I had sent him a care package, and staggered a couple of greeting cards through the mail, which he posted pictures of on his Facebook page. It all seemed like a lifetime ago.

The day before Rocky flew to Maryland he texted, asking me to login to Skype, and so I did.

"Hey. What's up?" I asked.

"Hey. So, I was thinking, and I just want you to let me finish before you say anything! Just hear me out," he said.

"Ok. What is it?" I asked.

"I want your unbiased advice *as a friend*," he reinforced.

"Ok! What is it?"

"I was thinking that maybe I should wait to have the talk with my wife when I come back home for good in December," he said.

"See, here you go again!" I said.

"Listen! Listen! Let me finish. The only reason I'm saying that is because I wanna be here just in case she tries something. At least if I'm here I can see what's going on," he explained.

"And then when December comes it'll be, 'Well, it's Christmas and I don't wanna do it so close to the holiday,' Then, it'll be New Years, then Valentine's Day. No!" I said.

"No, I won't. I'm not gonna say that. I just think I should wait until I'm home for good."

I had already spoken with my friend, Neequaye about everything that was going on, and he thought it was probably a better idea for Rocky to wait until he was home for good before he spoke with his wife. Otherwise, our trip to Dubai might be ruined if his wife didn't take the news well. Neequaye said that she might very well call him every day of our trip just to argue, so I agreed Rocky should wait.

"Ok, but, Rocky, December is my limit," I stressed.

"Ok, ok...Alright, let me go. I just wanted to talk to you about that. I need to run some errands and finish packing for tomorrow," he said.

"Alright," I said.

"I love you," he said.

"I love you too," I said.

En route to the airport to pick up Rocky, I stopped by a package store to grab a bottle of wine for a toast once we got to the hotel. I received a text message from Rocky just as I was leaving the store, and I was still fifteen minutes from BWI airport.

"Where are you?" he wrote.

"You landed??" I replied.

Rocky and I both wanted to be first at the airport to catch the first glimpse of each other since it was our first official meeting in person. I told Rocky that I would spot him in the airport before he had a chance to see me because I planned to be there waiting when he landed.

"LOL, no I'm hovering the city," he typed.

"Oh, LOL. I'm almost there. I'll see you first!" I replied.

"We'll see LOL," he wrote.

Rocky called my cell phone while I was parking.

"Hey, what do you have on?" he asked.

"Why?" I laughed.

"What do you have on?" he chuckled.

"You're at baggage claim already?" I asked.

I was reaching for the poster board that I had tucked on the back seat of the car. The day before, I had gone to an arts and crafts store to buy a few supplies to make a sign to hold up when Rocky came through the gate to baggage claim.

"Yeah, I don't see you. What do you have on?" he said laughing.

"Are you serious?" I asked laughing and running. "No, you're not!" I said.

I ran through the parking deck carrying the homemade sign. I had written his full name on the banner in large letters, but it was hyphenated with my last name.

When I arrived at the baggage carousel designated for his flight he wasn't there.

"Where are you? I'm here," I said panting.

"Huh?" he laughed.

"You heard me! Where are you?" I laughed.

"Boy, I just got off the plane. I'm walking to baggage claim," he laughed.

"You were still on the plane?" I laughed.

"Yeah, I was. I was just trying to see where you were," he laughed.

"Mmmhmm. What do you have on?" I asked.

"Why?" he laughed.

"Ok, you don't have to tell me. I'll see you when you get here," I laughed.

My heart raced. We had seen each other just about every day for six months on Skype, three to four hours at a time, but this was different. *What if the connection is lost in person? What if there's an awkward silence between us because we had nothing more to say? What if we didn't get along in person?*

As my mind wandered, I noticed Rocky descending the escalator. He was wearing taupe colored slacks, a fitted canary yellow V-neck sweater, and the cognac cap-toed, lace up, Gucci shoes he showed me online one day when we were on Skype.

Rocky had asked me a few months before to go into the Gucci store to try on a pair for him, so he would know which size he needed to order for himself because we wear the same size shoe. He wanted to order the shoes online while he was still in the Middle East, so he would have them when he arrived at home to the states.

Rocky looked away nervously when he saw me watching him coming towards me. I studied him, but I was smiling the entire time. We had joked about kissing in the airport when we saw each other, but I didn't really think he was serious. I forgot that I was holding the sign with his name. I held it up just before he was within arm's reach.

"Hey," he said smirking. "Your sign is upside down."

"Oh!" I said flipping it upright.

He hugged me then leaned in for a kiss, but I turned my head nervously, so he kissed my cheek.

"Oh, really?" he said.

"I didn't know you were really gonna do it," I said kissing his lips.

"I said I was gonna kiss you," he said.

"I didn't think you would really do it in the airport," I smiled.

"I don't know these people," he laughed.

We talked nervously as we walked to the car. I stole glances at him when he looked away, as did he. He was slightly taller than me, and more handsome in person than he was on Skype. Since Rocky had never been to Baltimore or Washington, D.C. before, I booked hotel reservations in both cities. The first night, we spent in D.C., but I took him for a seafood lunch in Lithicum Heights, Maryland.

From lunch we drove to D.C. and took a mini tour past the Washington mall before checking in to the Renaissance Hotel in DuPont Circle. I pulled into the driveway of the hotel and parked to unload our bags, and to check-in before parking the car.

Rocky took a seat in the hotel lobby with our bags while I checked us in.

"You wanna have a glass of wine in the lobby before we go up," he asked.

"Yeah, that's cool," I smiled.

"You want a red or white?" he asked.

"White. I'll have a Riesling," I said.

"Ok," he said walking to the hotel restaurant.

Rocky returned with two glasses of white wine as I finished up at the front desk.

"You wanna sit right here?" he asked.

"Yea, we can," I said.

Rocky and I took a seat in the lobby with our luggage surrounding us.

"Here's to us meeting," he said.

"...and a great trip," I added.

"Cheers," we said in unison.

Our conversation picked up at lunch, but the wine loosened us up, so there was more of a natural flow like we were used to having with each other.

"You wanna finish this upstairs?" he asked.

"Yeah, we can take it up. Let me grab a baggage cart," I said.

Rocky had several bags of luggage because he had packed for the three weeks that he would be in the U.S. I only had a weekend bag because my luggage for our weeklong vacation in Dubai was packed and waiting at my mother's house until we left the country on Sunday.

We took the elevator up to the room, and unloaded the bags from the cart.

"Ok, let me go back down to move the car. I'll be back," I said.

"Wait. I have something for you," he said reaching into one of his bags.

"What?"

"The first song you ever sent me was *Time After Time* by Cassandra Wilson," he said.

I remembered sending the song, but I hadn't remembered that it was the first song that I sent him when he asked me to put together a playlist for him while he was away.

"Ok," I said smiling.

"So, I wanted to give you something symbolic of time," he said.

Rocky pulled out a small Michael Kors shopping bag. When I reached inside, there was a small dark burl wood box, and inside the box was a gold watch adorned with a tortoise bracelet.

"Oh wow! Thank you," I said kissing his lips.

"Mmmhmm, you're welcome," he smiled.

"You didn't have to do this," I said looking at him and glancing back at the watch.

"I know, but I wanted to," he said.

"This is nice. I really appreciate this," I said still smiling.

"I knew you would. That's why I got it," he said.

The day before, when he was in a mall in Florida, Rocky had texted me a picture of the watch he was going to give me along with two others. He said that he was trying to decide which watch to buy for himself, but wanted my opinion. When he gave me the watch, I kissed him again, and raced downstairs to move the car.

I returned to the room to find Rocky in the shower, so I began unpacking. Rocky emerged from the shower and began parading around, wearing a devilish grin, and a pair of fitted boxer briefs. He laid face down on the bed with his arms folded under his head. I wanted to taste him. I crawled on him, fully dressed, and kissed his lower back and licked the center of his back up to his traps.

"Mmm," he moaned.

I kissed and slid my tongue along the nape of his neck, and sucked on his ear. His body curled into a fetal position. I ran my hand along the inside of his thigh to his crotch, then reached in his underwear. Rocky rolled over onto his back and extended his legs in the air vertically, so that I could remove his underwear. I pulled on his underwear as he wiggled his body out of them.

His underwear finally slipped from under his butt, and I pulled them up past his thighs, his knees, shins and from around his ankles. I licked and kissed his v-line, then slid my tongue down to the crevice of his inner thigh as his body trembled. Rocky lifted his legs and rested them on my shoulders. I licked the seam of his scrotum, then slipped my tongue inside him. I kissed and licked on it, around it, and inside him.

Rocky grabbed my face to stop me, but I sucked his fingers, then licked and kissed the palm of his hand.

"Ahhh shit," he moaned.

I sucked my middle finger, then rubbed it on his anus. Rocky was wet, so I pressed the tip of my dick on his ass.

"Aaahh…babe wait. Let's get the test," he begged.

Rocky and I had agreed that we would test ourselves together for HIV before we had sex, so he had brought along two HIV home tests.

"Ok, where are they?" I asked.

"In my bag," he said.

I crawled off the bed and grabbed the tests, and together we opened the packages. Then we swabbed our cheeks and placed our test sticks in the solution. I set my test on one side of the room, and Rocky placed his near the television so we wouldn't mix up the two.

"Well, I can jump in the shower 'cause they take twenty minutes," I said.

"All right," he said.

After I showered we checked the HIV test results, and they were both negative. But, instead of having sex we got dressed and walked three blocks to the Fireplace, a neighborhood bar.

After a couple of drinks, we anxiously rushed back to the hotel to escape the winter air.

We began kissing and ripping our clothes off the moment we crossed the threshold to the room. We lay naked on the bed with our bodies tangled together and Rocky's legs wrapped around my waist. My fingers danced along his stomach and navel as I kissed his lips softly.

"Did you wait for me?" I whispered.

"Mmmhmm," he mumbled with his eyes closed.

"You didn't give it to nobody?" I asked softly.

"Nope," he mumbled flashing a slight smile.

"You sure?" I whispered.

"Mmmmhmmm," he moaned.

I hooked my arm around Rocky's body and pulled him closer to me, and slowly entered him.

It was nearly eleven o'clock at night, and we needed to eat. We hadn't eaten since lunch after we left the airport. We got dressed and headed to Bus Boys and Poets in Northwest D.C. at 14th and V streets. Rocky fell in love with Busboy's that night, and I was falling in love with him.

Saturday morning, we had brunch at Bread and Chocolate, a neighborhood bakery, referred to us by the hotel concierge. After that, we drove to the White House and the Martin Luther King Jr. Memorial to take pictures.

"Can I hold your hand?" Rocky laughed.

"Stop playing," I laughed.

Rocky slowly reached for my hand as we walked in front of The White House.

"Ok, that's enough!" he said pulling his hand back quickly.

"So silly," I laughed.

Rocky and I walked back to the car so we could drive to Baltimore. We planned to check in to the Renaissance Harborplace Hotel, make a stop at my mother's house to eat, then go to the gym for a quick workout.

I pointed out the Aquarium, the World Trade Center and a few other landmarks at the Inner Harbor for Rocky once we made it to Baltimore, and I shared a few childhood memories with him too. Rocky wanted to venture over to the shops at Harborplace, but we checked into the hotel then headed to my mom's, and decided to visit the shops later in the evening.

Rocky was still wearing his wedding band when we parked outside of my mom's house.

"You might wanna take your wedding ring off before we go inside," I said.

"Ok," he answered.

I didn't see Rocky remove the ring, but I noticed that it was gone as we entered my mother's living room. When we walked in the house I could see my mother and sister standing in the kitchen, reflected in the floor to ceiling mirrors that covered the living and dining room walls.

"Come on in here! Don't be acting shy!" Donnie shouted.

"Hello, how are you?" Rocky said walking towards the kitchen.

"Mmm, you are *so* handsome," my sister said as she hugged him.

"Well, thank you," he smiled.

"How was your flight?" she asked.

"Long!" he laughed.

"How long is that flight?" she asked.

"Like fourteen hours."

"Oh gracious! I won't be going there. That's too long to be on a plane," she said.

"Hey Rocky," my mom said walking towards him for a hug.

"Hi, there. It's good to finally meet you," he said leaning down for a hug.

Rocky had also spoken to my mom several times over Skype. Whenever we needed to discuss something privately, and my mom was in the room with me, we used the instant messenger feature on Skype.

"Are you hungry?" she asked Rocky.

"Yeah, a little. Craig and I are going to the gym, so I don't wanna eat too much," he said.

"Oh, Lord. He act like he can't miss that gym," Donnie said.

"No, I wanna go," Rocky replied.

"Well Craig, fix Rocky something to eat," my mother said.

I whipped up a quick brunch for us that we scarfed down before we ran up to my bedroom to change into our gym clothes.

After the gym, Rocky and I were ready to eat again. His cell phone rang as we parked in the parking lot of the restaurant. It was Rocky's wife calling.

"This is my wife calling. Let me take this. I'll be in in a second," he said.

"Ok," I answered.

Rocky's wife was under the impression that he had returned to the Middle East the day he left Florida, but in actuality he flew to see me instead. So, my guess was that she was calling to see that he had made it back overseas safely.

There was only one other instance I could recall that his wife had called in the past, and that was while we were on Skype. But, even in that instance, Rocky simply put me on hold and muted his computer because their calls were always brief, and this time was no different. Before I could decide what I would order for lunch, Rocky was standing beside me.

After lunch, Rocky and I headed back downtown to get a nap because we had plans to meet that night with my cousins for drinks, and he and I were going out to a couple of gay bars in Baltimore.

Sunday morning, we attended the eleven o'clock service at The Empowerment Temple. After church, Rocky and I purchased sweatpants to wear on the flight, extra underwear for the trip, and a few other essentials from Marshall's. My mom picked up chitterlings from Lexington Market for Rocky's lunch, which they had discussed the day before. I chose Popeye's chicken with red beans & rice.

My dad agreed to take us to the airport, and he arrived at my mom's house just as we were finishing our lunch. Rocky and

I piled our luggage into my dad's car, and I hugged my mom goodbye. My brother Jimmy pulled Rocky off to the side.

"Ehh man. You make sure you look out for my brother over there. Don't let nothing happen to him," he said.

"All right," Rocky said, shaking Jimmy's hand.

"Y'all have a safe flight. Call me when you get there," my mother added.

"I'll send you an email. There won't be no phone calls," I laughed.

"Well, whichever," she said.

Although Rocky had been in the U.S. for two weeks he was still jetlagged. He was asleep ten minutes into the drive to the airport, and didn't wake up until we were at the airport.

15 DUBAI

Rocky and I landed at Dubai International airport in the early evening of October 27th. I was exhausted from the flight because I couldn't seem to get comfortable on the plane. Rocky and I took turns using each other as pillows, so I was able to doze off several times on the flight, but never slept consistently. I was awakened by the in-flight crew delivering meals and beverages, to use the restroom, or by the passenger seated next to us who needed to use the restroom.

Rocky suggested that we pack snacks for the flight to have something to munch on in between the meals, and because he said the food wasn't the best. By the time we landed in Dubai, I was starving because, as he said, the food was tasteless. So after we retrieved our bags in the terminal, we picked up sandwiches to-go from one of the restaurants in the airport—we were both eager to get to the hotel to shower and relax.

There was complete mayhem outside the airport as we tried to hail a taxi, and it was sweltering hot. Rocky got a cab and directed the driver to the Holiday Inn Express Jumeirah. In the brief car ride to the hotel I noticed that most of the cars on the road were high-end luxury or sports cars, and the homes were mansion-style compounds. The architecture, in this desert city, was reminiscent of Aruba or Las Vegas.

To my surprise, the Holiday Inn was lavish in comparison to the hotel brand in the states, but everything in Dubai was luxe. Hotel staff welcomed Rocky and me the moment we pulled up to the hotel in the taxi. The driver directed us to the front desk while he gathered our luggage from the car, and the front desk clerks welcomed us with five star treatment.

It was after ten o'clock at night when we finally made it to our room. I unpacked my laptop first because I had promised Kepri that I would FaceTime her once Rocky and I were settled in the room. With the eight-hour time difference I knew she would still be in her office at Essence magazine.

"Hiiii," Kepri smiled.

"Hey!" I said smiling.

"Hello," Rocky added.

I was sitting in between Rocky's legs in the lonely chair that's always pushed up to a desk in every hotel room. Rocky and I shared the tiny screen on my iPhone.

"Awww, Craig, I'm so happy for you. I'm happy for both of you!" she said beaming.

"Thank you," I smiled.

"Craig, you look so happy. You deserve it," she added.

"I am happy," I turned to look at Rocky.

Rocky looked at me and pecked my lips.

"I know that's right!" Kepri laughed. "Isn't he *even more* handsome in person?" she asked.

"Mmmhmm," I said.

"I'm talking to Rocky *about* you!" she said.

"Oh," I laughed.

"Yes, he is," Rocky laughed, too.

"All right, well, get some rest. I need to get back to work," she laughed.

"Ok," I said.

"Nice meeting you," Rocky said.

"You too Rocky! Hopefully, I'll get to meet you in person someday. Craig stay in the moment. I love you," she smiled.

"I will. I love you too," I smiled.

There were no secrets between Kepri and me, so of course she knew that Rocky was married, and that was her way of telling me not to over-think things because I wasn't in good practice of talking myself *off* the ledge.

Because we were exhausted from the flight, we decided to stay in the first night to rest and then venture out the next day to the Mall of the Emirates.

Later, instead of sending a regular email to my mother, I opted to send her a video message. I positioned my laptop so that Rocky and I could both be seen on the screen.

"Hey, Ma," I said.

"Hello! Wish you were here with us," Rocky said.

"It's 11:40 in the morning here. We just got some food. Oh, we're going skiing today—" I told her.

"But first I gotta tell you," Rocky laughed. "The people forgot to give us our wake up call this morning, so Craig called down there," he laughed.

"So, of course, we're eating for free!" We both laughed. "But, when we leave here we're going skiing. I don't know what we'll do for the rest of the day. But, I just wanted to say I love you. I'll talk to you later," I said.

"Byyyee," Rocky added.

Rocky had an itinerary of things for us to do for the week, so we got dressed and took a car to the Mall of the Emirates. The initial plan as I told my mom in the video message, was to go snowboarding at Ski Dubai, an indoor ski resort with an indoor ski area. It's a part of the Mall of the Emirates, one of the largest shopping malls in the world. However, we were forced to reschedule our snowboarding session for the next day because the time slots that we wanted were all filled.

Instead of skiing, we toured the 700-plus-store mall. Afterwards, Rocky took me to dinner at an African restaurant also located in the mall. Later that evening, Rocky and I strolled down to Jumeirah Beach, a three-block walk from our hotel. On the way, we spotted a hookah lounge and a Baskin Robbins ice cream shop that we planned to stop in on the way back to the hotel.

There were only a few people on the beach. The sky was pitch black as we crossed the sand on our way to the ocean, but the temperature still hovered at the 90-degree mark.

"There's no way around it now. I have to tell her," Rocky said softly.

Out of the blue, Rocky acknowledged what was happening between us, and there was no denying that we both felt it. We were beyond the point of just a fling.

"Let's get in the water," I said looking at him.

It seemed we were the only people in the water that night, but I could see a few people on the sand through the darkness in the distance. It was easy for us to be affectionate in the privacy of our hotel room, but we were very mindful not to be demonstrative in public. But, once we disappeared into the ocean darkness, Rocky jumped into my arms and wrapping his legs around my waist.

"Hold me up. Jump over the waves, but don't let the water knock us over. The first time we fall, I'm getting down," he laughed.

"I got you! We ain't falling," I said leaping the huge waves.

"Here comes another one. Get ready to jump. Ok, jump!" he warned.

"You know these shorts are too little, right?" I laughed.

"Leave my shorts alone. I like my shorts," he laughed.

"You can't even pull them all the way up," I said kissing his neck.

Rocky wrapped his arms around my neck.

"You think they can see us?" he asked.

"No, it's dark as hell out here. Ain't really nobody out here, but us," I answered.

"Oh, here comes a big ass wave," he said.

By then, my legs were too tired to jump and the wave towered over us, forcing us under water.

"Ok, that's it! I'm done," Rocky laughed.

"All right, let's go," I laughed.

Before we returned to the hotel, we stopped in the ice cream shop to satisfy Rocky's sweet tooth, so by the time we turned in that night we were drained.

Rocky was adamant that he didn't snore when he slept, and for the most part it was true. However, that night, he must have been exhausted when he drifted off to sleep because he was snoring. I wanted to record him as proof, but I wasn't sure I'd be able to get to my cell phone because Rocky was cuddled up so close to me in the bed.

My cell phone rested next to the bed on the nightstand. I carefully reached for it, but the second that I moved, Rocky moved. I waited a couple minutes to try again. I was able to grab the phone, and held it above us, then hit record.

"Babe," I whispered.

Huh," he mumbled in his sleep.

I chuckled because I didn't expect him to hear me, but his response was perfect for the video.

"You're snoring right now and I can't get to sleep," I whispered.

Rocky flinched a bit when the light from the cell phone flashed on his face, so I stopped recording just for a moment until he settled back into sleep. Then I continued recording.

"I had to get this on camera since you don't believe you *ever* snore. I'll show you this in the morning," I whispered.

The next morning, while we were lying in bed I showed Rocky the video.

"Babe, look at this," I said laughing.

Rocky was still buried under the covers, so I pulled the sheet back from his face and pressed play.

"What is that?" He squinted at the screen.

"Just watch," I laughed.

Rocky was still trying to make out the video because it was very dark and grainy.

"That's us. Listen," I said.

He listened for a moment, then laughed.

"You make me sick."

"But you don't snore though," I chuckled.

"I was tired, hell," he laughed.

During the remaining days of the trip Rocky, and I made up for the first day that we stayed in to rest. We frequented a shisha lounge for drinks and flavored hookah, and we finally snowboarded at the Mall of the Emirates, visited the Dubai mall, and spent a full day in the water park at the Atlantis Dubai where I swam with the dolphins.

Rocky stood by to photograph and film me swimming with the dolphins because he swam with the dolphins on his first visit to Atlantis. Hence the pictures I saw on his profile when we met. But the video of me swimming with the dolphins wasn't the only video we made. Rocky and I made a series of memory videos, which also included video footage from all of our excursions, for us to keep so we could one day look back on them for memories' sake.

"I hope you know that I'm really stepping out of my comfort zone with you," Rocky said.

"What do you mean?" I asked.

"Just being on video with you is a big step," he said.

"I get that, but I'm also well beyond my comfort zone too. You're not alone," I said.

By the end of every day we were ready to crash, thanks to the desert heat, and the going and going nonstop. For some reason Rocky was always asleep before me with his body nestled under mine. Usually I lay there watching him sleep, kissing his lips and daydreaming about a life with him—imagining that week together as a permanent thing, and not just a weeklong getaway.

I pulled away from Rocky to get my laptop because I wanted to send him an email that he would find randomly at some point during the trip. And, I wanted to take us back to how we began—email.

Rocky,

You're lying under me sleeping as I'm typing this email. It's a beautiful picture to see, but since I'm awake and you aren't I figured I'd send this quick note. I'm thinking of how special this moment is. I can't say enough about how appreciative I am to have you this close to me—physically and emotionally.

I'm still blown away by the watch you gave me, and the symbolism behind it. Even more, that I'm in Dubai with you because you 'made shit happen.' Thank you.

Know that I appreciate you and all the little things…You have a kind heart. You're thoughtful, and you have a beautiful spirit.

I'm really grateful that we can always talk things thru to clarity. With that, I'm present. I'm in the moment with you. I don't want us to scare ourselves away from what may be the best either of us has ever had or seen before.

I'm shocked that I haven't said I love you in a few days. So, I want you to know that I love you. Not only do I love you, but also I love the man I met on Skype, the man I've had the pleasure of sharing the last few days with, and the man I've been making love to.

Me

When I woke up the next morning Rocky was crawling back on the bed towards me.

"Good morning. I got your email. That was sweet. Thank you," he smiled then kissed my lips.

"You're welcome," I smiled.

On my last day in Dubai, we spent the better part of the day in the hotel talking—reflecting on our week together, before my evening flight. I wasn't looking forward to the fourteen-hour flight back to the States, nor was I ready to be apart from Rocky again. The week had flashed by.

On the bright side, Rocky was coming home permanently in just six short weeks, but we still lived in two different cities. I was overwhelmed trying to figure out how the pieces to this puzzle would fall into place.

Rocky was equally sad that I was leaving although he wasn't as vocal about it as I was. He tried to cover up his feelings, but I caught a few tears falling from his eyes.

"Ahh, are you crying?" I smiled.

"I think something is in my eye," he said walking in the restroom.

"Yeah, tears," I laughed. "Come here, it's ok to cry. I'm sad too. Come here, let me see," I said.

"No," he hesitated. "I hate that I cry so easily," he added.

Rocky claimed that his tears were the result of a surprise wedding that was airing on television, but I knew he was just as melancholy as I was about being apart again.

Rocky took the taxi with me back to the airport and walked me to the security checkpoint. There were tears in both of our eyes. We stood at the gate hugging and fighting back the tears that were close to falling.

"I really had a good time," he said.

"I did too. Thank you for everything," I smiled.

"Email me when you get back," he said.

"I will. I love you," I said.

"I love you too," he responded. "Ok, you gotta go so you won't miss your flight," he said.

"All right," I said.

I turned to look back a few times to watch him leaving, and each time I looked he was also turning back to look. We waved one final time as I passed by the security wall. A few tears streamed down my face once I was seated on the plane.

Instinctively, I knew things would somehow be different between us once Rocky was home for good. My tears were a mixture of sadness, and grief because I knew that I was mourning a love that would be lost.

16 BENDING ЯULES

The flight from Dubai was an hour longer because we were traveling against the wind, but it felt dramatically longer because I flew solo. My mother was waiting for me outside of BWI airport when I landed.

"Hey Craig," she said.

"Hey," I said solemnly.

"What's wrong with you?" she asked.

"Nothing," I mumbled.

"Well, how was the trip?"

"It was good. I had a good time," I said looking out the window of her car.

"When does Rocky go back to work?" she asked.

"He flies back to Afghanistan today," I said.

Rocky worked mostly in Dubai, but he also had assignments in Afghanistan. Immediately following our trip he was scheduled to be in Afghanistan.

"And when does he come home for good?" she asked.

"December," I said.

"Well, that's not too long," she said.

"No," I mumbled.

"What, are you sad?" she asked.

"Yeah. I didn't wanna leave," I admitted.

"Well, I'm sure he's just as sad," she said.

"He is," I said. "He cried...I haven't felt like this in a long time. But, it's not just that, we live in two different cities. I can't see how this could work."

"Well, you could always go there and stay for a while to see how things go, and if that works you could move there," she offered.

My mom knew that Rocky had a home in Florida, but she still wasn't aware of the complexities. He was married, so it wasn't that simple. Every now and then she would ask who was watching over his home while he was away, but I always brushed off the question.

"He asked me before if I would move there, but I can't move to Florida," I said.

"Why not?" she asked.

"'Cause."

"'Cause what?" she asked.

"'Cause I don't wanna move into someone else's house because if things don't go right the first thing they say is, 'get out!'" I explained.

After moving into Carrington's condo many years before I promised myself that I wouldn't put myself in the position to be asked to leave again because it wasn't *our* home.

"I don't think he's the kind to do that," my mother said.

"How do you know?" I quizzed.

"I don't know. I just don't think he is though," she said.

"Mmm," I said.

"Well, you can get your own apartment for six months, then move in," she said.

"I'm not doing that. If I move to Florida we need to live together. I'm not renting a place—that would defeat the purpose of me moving," I said.

"Well, you'll figure it out when that time comes," she said.

I received an email notification on my cell phone—it was an email from Rocky.

Hey Babe,

I really do hope the trip was more than you expected. I was sad after you left, but I'll be ok.

I'm so glad we had the opportunity to get to know more of each other. Coming to your city was so awesome. You showed me a wonderful time. You coming here was just icing on the cake. It was also an opportunity for me to let you into more of my world.

I'm in the airport right now getting ready to head to Afghanistan. I wanted to send you this email so that you'd get it as soon as you arrive back home. I will forever remember both trips and how great you made me feel. I only hope I made you feel just as good.

I love you and I will write you again once I get settled in. I pray your flight was a safe one.

ONE THING FOR CERTAIN, TWO THINGS FOR SURE

Rocky

*****

It was time for Rocky to come home for good in December
of 2013, so we planned a second visit together in Maryland and
D.C. This time around, Rocky came to see me before going home
to Florida. His family, as well as his wife, was of the belief that he
was still in the Middle East when he was actually spending the
weekend with me.

Rocky wanted to split his visit again; part of the time in
Baltimore and part in D.C., so I reserved a different hotel at
Baltimore's Inner Harbor as well as one in D.C. to give him
another experience in both cities.

This trip was intended to be a bit more relaxed, and not as
regimented so we didn't make any special plans this trip. I invited
a few family members over to my mom's the evening Rocky
arrived to have a few drinks with us, and to play spades. Earlier
that same day, I checked into the hotel in Baltimore to set up a
few surprises for Rocky. I laid out a pair of my bikini underwear
on the bed, along with a bottle of his favorite cognac. I also set up
an e-vite that would notify him of a movie date once we got to D.C.
the next day to see the movie, *The Best Man Holiday*.

However, my plans for the day that he arrived were
preempted because Rocky missed his connecting flight due to a
delay, which meant he didn't arrive in Maryland until close to
midnight. When I arrived, the airport was deserted, with the

exception of those of us waiting to greet the last planes arriving. I waited eagerly for Rocky outside of the security gate as several passengers passed by me. He finally appeared carrying two oversized duffel bags, and a look of discontent on his face that slowly turned to a smile when he saw me.

"I am so tired," he said with a smile, kissing my lips.

I noticed an older Black woman standing by watching our exchange with a smile.

"I know you are," I smiled.

I grabbed one of Rocky's bags to carry for him.

"I should have taken my ass straight home. I knew this flight was gonna give me problems," he said.

"We've lost a whole day, but I'm glad you came," I said.

"Uggh," he groaned.

"You hungry?" I asked.

"Yes, but I just wanna get to the hotel," he answered.

"I figured, so I brought you some food…I had a whole day planned. We were gonna have dinner and play cards at my mom's with my cousins—the ones that you met," I said.

"Are we going to D.C. tonight?" he asked.

"No," I said.

"Ok, good 'cause I'm tired."

"I almost booked the hotel in D.C. for tonight. I'm glad I didn't. Plus, tomorrow is the night to go to Bus Boys and Poets," I explained.

I thought Rocky would be ready for bed once we made it to the hotel, but he wasn't. He wanted to pop open the cognac I bought him, and have a few drinks in the hotel courtyard. It was freezing outside, so we bundled up and sat in the courtyard until the cold was unbearable, and we could no longer fight sleep.

The one thing that Rocky wanted to do on this trip was have dinner at Bus Boys and Poets in D.C. again, but I managed to introduce him to Mt. Vernon Stable, my favorite rib spot in Maryland, and then karaoke at Grand Central Club, which partially redeemed the bumpy start of our visit.

Rocky told me that he and his wife were spending the Christmas holiday with his family in Charlotte because his mom hosted an annual holiday party. I was preparing to spend the week of Christmas in a cabin with my family in Deep Creek Lake in Maryland. I was slightly agitated that Rocky was still planning to spend the Christmas holiday with his wife, in his hometown, because that was their routine, and that could send mixed messages to her. It seemed to me that, if he really planned to put things in motion to leave the marriage, he would have had the discussion instead of continuing the tradition.

However, Rocky insisted that he would have the talk with his wife while they were in Charlotte because he wanted to be close to his family after the talk, but I was skeptical. Once Rocky went home to Florida, I noticed right away that he wasn't as available as he once was. He called me on Skype a few times while his wife was in another room, using earphones to keep our conversation private, but we no longer had the luxury of speaking freely when we wanted on the phone, and for as long as we wanted.

Rocky called me randomly when he was home alone in Charlotte at his mom's house, or when his wife was out. He even texted randomly to say how much he loved me, and to ask what my family and I were doing while at the cabin. But it began to feel like we were sneaking around, and more importantly, that he was ok with us moving about clandestinely.

With that realization, I slowly began to let go. I wanted to love Rocky through that phase in his life, but changing his circumstances was something he had to do for himself. He had to choose the life he wanted, not the life I wanted for him or for us.

Rocky lost the nerve again to have the talk with his wife while they were in Charlotte. Finally, on December 31, 2013, I faced the harsh reality that Rocky loved me the best he knew how, but it wasn't enough for me.

When Rocky called, I knew that it would be a conversation that would change everything for us. I was at home with my mom when he called, but I stepped out of the room to take the call.

"I think I should try to work on my marriage because I haven't really tried. Things might be different with us...now that I'm home," he said.

"Rocky, she didn't stand a chance from the beginning. She would never have your heart because you're attracted to men. Being home is only gonna prove that," I said.

"I know that I wanna be with you, but I don't wanna keep starting over," he said.

"You *knew* this day would eventually come! Where did you think this was headed...all of the conversations, the trips? What did you think the end was gonna be? You didn't see this day coming?" I asked.

"I know, I know, I know. I'm just confused," he said.

"*Confused?* You're not confused! You're weak! You *know* what you want!" I shouted.

"I know what I said when I was in the Middle East, but it's different now that I'm home," he replied.

"You did all that talking when you were overseas and now you're confused?" I yelled. "I knew this shit was gonna happen!"

"I haven't really given my marriage a try. Sometimes I feel like I can make my marriage work, but then I know how I feel about you," he said.

I couldn't believe what he was saying.

"Rocky, you're gay! What's there to work on? You said yourself that you can't even have sex with her. Why are you lying to yourself?"

"Are you gonna let me finish?" he asked.

But I couldn't stop myself.

"All those times I tried to pull away to give you space so you could decide for yourself and you begged me to hold on—to wait for you! And now you're confused? Listen, I'm not gonna beg you to be with me! I'm not about to campaign for this because I don't have to!" I shouted.

"I'm not asking you to campaign," he said.

"I wanna be with somebody who knows who they are— who knows what they want," I said.

"Craig—" he said.

"Don't call me! Don't Skype me! Don't email me, and don't text me! I'm done!" I shouted.

"Are you serious?" he asked.

"Yes!"

"I know I'm making a mistake…I'm gonna regret this for the rest of my life," he sighed.

"But that's the choice you're making. I gotta go," I said.

"Are you hanging up?" he asked.

"Yeah, I don't have anything else to say. Bye," I said as I released the call.

I was angry with Rocky, but I was furious with myself because I knew better. I knew, when we met, that I should've stepped back and allowed him to deal with himself and his marriage before getting involved with him.

A text message from Rocky came through a moment after we hung up.

"I feel so stupid," he wrote.

I ignored his text, then deleted all of our past text conversations as well as his phone number from my contacts. I even logged into Facebook and Skype to delete him as a contact. I didn't want any contact with him, and I wasn't going to wrestle with him about his reality.

Marriage, in Rocky's mind, was his only chance at happily ever after—longevity. He believed it was impossible for two men to have a long-term relationship void of deception and game playing. Rocky's first relationship had a lot to do with how he saw men and gay relationships. His first *gay* relationship, as with many of us, set the tone for the way he approached love with other men.

Three days passed without talking to Rocky. It was the longest we had ever gone without communicating in some way. I wanted to talk to him and I wondered if he was having a hard time *not* talking to me, but I was adamant about not calling. If he wanted to be with me he would have to show it, not tell me.

A short while later, I got a call from a number that I didn't recognize. Typically I don't answer calls from phone numbers that I don't know, but I answered because it was a Georgia area code.

"Hello," I said.

"Hi. May I speak to Craig?" said a voice I didn't recognize.

"This is Craig," I answered.

"Uh, hi, this is Gerald, Rocky's brother," the caller said nervously.

"Hi," I said.

"Rocky asked me to call you to see how you're doing?"

"He asked you to call me to see how I'm doing?" I repeated.

"Yeah, I didn't wanna get in the middle of this 'cause that's not what I do, but he begged me to call you because he said you would know that he was sincere if I called you," he explained.

I was taken aback because I had no idea that Rocky's brother knew about me. I would've expected a call from Rocky's sister because he had told her about us while he was still living and working in the Middle East. His sister encouraged him to live his life. She also said that she never expected his marriage to last, and that she never understood why he and his wife married because she *knew* that he was gay, and had suspicions that his wife was a lesbian.

I had also questioned his wife's sexuality after snooping around on his Facebook page when we first met. When I first asked Rocky if he thought his wife was gay he dismissed it, but later he told me that she had been in love with a female officer while they were dating. But despite it all, Rocky hadn't told his brother any of this until he went home to Charlotte for Christmas with his wife, so this phone call was a complete shock for me.

"I'm all right, but I've been better. I'm pissed off with him. I just don't understand what happened. What did he tell you? Did he tell you everything?" I asked.

I didn't want to share more with Rocky's brother than he had.

"Yeah, he told me you guys met about eight months ago and that you cared a lot about each other. He told me part of the story when he came home for Christmas. He stopped by my house to talk, and then he called me when he went home. I guess after y'all talked the other day," he explained.

"Ok," I said.

"Man, my brother was devastated when you broke it off. I've never heard him cry like that," he said.

"He was crying?" I asked.

"Yeah. He said that this wasn't how he wanted things to turn out," Rocky's brother explained.

"Then he should've done what he said he was gonna to do! Did he tell you that he came to visit me in Maryland twice, and I flew with him to Dubai for a week?" I quizzed.

"Yeah, he told me all that," the brother responded. "I really don't know why he felt like he had to get married. He told my mom and the rest of us when we were kids. I don't know what he's afraid of. I told him straight up that he needs to leave that marriage because it's not fair to her, and he can't give her what she needs."

"And she can't give him what he needs," I added.

"Right. I don't know if he won't leave because they spent all that money on the wedding or because they just got married a year ago, and they're worried about what people will think, but I just want my brother to be happy. Man, my brother is awesome and I just want the best for him," he said.

"Well, he told me that he's worried about your mom," I said.

"Yeah, my mom is real traditional so it may take her a minute, but she'll come around. But as far as the rest of the family, we're cool," he said.

Gerald also said that he knew about Rocky's ten-year relationship. He told me that he had spoken on the phone with Rocky's partner a time or two, but they never met in person. Although they lived in different states I still felt it was strange that Rocky kept his family and his partner separate for ten years.

"I mean, he kept telling me to hold on every time I pulled away, and to trust that he was gonna leave his marriage when he came home, but he choked. I mean, I introduced him to my family and now I feel like a fool," I said.

"Look, my brother is gay, not bisexual. Man, I saw how he looks at other guys when we're at the gym working out. He may think I don't see him looking or the way they look at him, but I see them trying to get his attention. And, I told him flat out, 'If you don't work this out with Craig you ain't gon do nothing but try to make another connection with somebody else," he said.

"Right. Well, I did my part. I don't know what else to say or do about it," I said.

"I'mma keep talking to him. That's one thing about me and my brother, we can be honest with each other because we are so close. I was kinda in a similar situation when me and my wife separated and I had to make a decision. But, I'mma tell him just like I'm telling you...I just feel bad for both of you 'cause I can tell that you care a lot about each other. But I'll talk to him and get back to you," he said.

"Ok, you can tell him to call me," I said.

"Ok, Craig. Good talking to you man."

"You too."

The next day Rocky called me.

"Hello," I said.

"Hey," he said.

"How are you?" I asked.

"I'm ok."

"So, I guess you know I spoke with your brother yesterday," I said.

"Yeah, I asked him to call you for me," he said

Rocky explained that he started filling his brother in about us when he and his wife were in Charlotte visiting for Christmas.

"I almost didn't call you," he admitted.

"Why?"

"Because I felt so stupid. And I didn't want to drag you into the New Year with all this. I didn't think that was fair to you...I figured I would just take care of this first then call you once I'm out of my marriage" he said.

"Mmm,' I mumbled.

"Craig, I never wanted to hurt you. I hope you know that I really care about you—that I love you. I don't think you could ever doubt that. I've always shown you that," he said.

"I don't doubt how you feel. I just don't understand how you're able to walk away so easily like we had nothing. I can't imagine walking away from you because of fear...It's just hard for me to believe that fear could *ever* eclipse love," I said.

"Craig, I'm not as strong as you, but every day I get stronger. Every day I get more courage to say a little more to her, but it's a lot harder than I thought it would be. I don't wanna hurt her. I keep thinking about the look on her face when I tell her," he confessed.

"But, what are you gonna feel when I'm with someone else?" I asked.

Rocky hesitated.

"I won't like it, but I'll have to deal with it. I honestly believe if it's really meant for us to be together there's nothing that can stop that from happening," he said.

"That's a chance I would never take with you," I said.

"I was devastated the other day when we got off the phone," he admitted.

"Your brother told me, but I would've never known that had he not told me. I felt like you just put your feelings in the back of a drawer and closed it. You hide your feelings from me," I said.

"I just have a different way of handling things. After we got off the phone I thought about you constantly. I wondered what you were doing, and I knew if you were on my mind heavily that I had to be on yours too. I mean, there were times I almost called you while I was in the bed with her 'cause I just wanted to talk to you," he said.

"So, why torture yourself?" I asked. "The longer you wait the more difficult it's gonna be for you, and even more painful for her. It's not gonna get any easier."

"I'm taking my car to the dealer to get service. Let's talk on Skype when I get back to the house," he said.

"Ok," I said.

That night, Rocky called me on Skype from his home patio. He said his wife was inside. It was the first time we had seen each other since he came to visit me in Maryland a month before.

"Hey," he said smiling.

I smiled back at him.

"Hey, what's up?"

"It's good to see you."

"You too."

"You look good," he said.

"You do too. Seems like I haven't seen you in forever," I said.

"I know right?...I miss you," he said.

"Do something about it then."

Rocky beamed at me through the screen.

"I want you to come to Tallahassee."

"Come to Tallahassee?" I quizzed.

"Yeah," he smiled.

"How am I gonna come to Tallahassee? Am I supposed to stay in a hotel and wait for you to sneak out to come see me?" I asked.

"No, she's going out of town for work for like five days," he smiled.

"Oh, my God...You're still—" I said.

"Can you just go with it and say yes," he interjected

"Oh, my God," I sighed. "When?"

"Next week. I have to get the exact dates, but I'll let you know, so we can get the plane ticket," he said.

"Ok, but we're not staying in your house," I said firmly.

Rocky didn't respond at first, so I said it again.

"*We're not staying in that house!*" I said.

"Ok!" he said smiling.

"I'll book a hotel downtown...Just because I don't know her doesn't mean I can't respect her," I said.

"Alright, well, let me go back inside. I'll call you tomorrow...I love you," he added.

"I love you too," I said.

On the day I was scheduled to go, I felt indifferent about going to Tallahassee. Rocky called me on Skype after he dropped his wife off at the airport. I was still in bed and my flight was scheduled to leave in three hours.

"What are you still doing in the bed? Don't you need to be on your way to the airport?" he asked.

"I'm about to get up in a few minutes," I said.

"You need to get up before you miss the flight," he insisted.

"I'm already packed. It's not gonna take that long to get to the airport," I said.

"Ok, don't miss the flight," he said.

"All right, let me get up and get ready. I'll text you when I'm on the plane," I said.

"Ok," Rocky answered.

I tossed a few last minute items in my suitcase, and dashed to the airport.

Rocky picked me up from the airport just hours after he took his wife, so this was his second trip to the airport in one day. His wife left on a morning flight, and I touched down on an afternoon flight. Rocky pulled up a few minutes after I arrived. I was waiting outside when he pulled up in his convertible BMW with the top down.

"You giving me a kiss here too?" I asked jokingly.

"Hell no. Not in Tallahassee," he laughed.

"You don't know everybody here."

"Unh onh."

"So, I booked a Marriott downtown. You have your stuff with you?" I continued.

Rocky had a smirk on his face.

"I need to run by the house real quick," he said.

"For what? I don't need to see the house," I said.

"We're not staying in a hotel when we can stay at my house for free," he smiled.

"I told you before I came that I didn't want to stay in your house."

Rocky continued driving, and before long we were pulling into his driveway.

It was eerie being in his house because he had taken me on a virtual tour on Skype, and because I couldn't escape the feeling of being caught. I kept anticipating his wife coming home early unexpectedly. But he didn't seem to understand my discomfort.

"You can come all the way in. Make yourself comfortable," he said.

"This is terrible...We're not sleeping in your bedroom. We can at least sleep in the guest room," I said.

"That's fine," he smiled.

"You ain't gon have me fucking in your bed," I mumbled to myself.

Rocky and I settled on his patio around the fire pit. He puffed on a black & mild cigar, and we both relaxed with a cocktail. Rocky had stopped smoking cigarettes before we met because I told him that I wouldn't date a smoker. Occasionally, he smoked a black & mild, but it was rare.

"Why did you want me to come here?" I asked.

"Because I missed you. I wanted to see you. It wasn't for sex or nothing like that," he answered.

"Have you thought about what happened?" I asked.

"I think about it every day. There's not a day that passes that I don't think about you. But let's talk about something else. I don't wanna talk about that," he said.

"You never do," I said.

There was still a crisp in the air that night, so we retired to the guest bedroom. Rocky excused himself to the master bedroom to shower, and I showered in the guest bathroom and then climbed into bed.

Rocky returned to the guest room naked. I lay on the bed watching him lotion his body. He crawled onto the bed, then straddled me. Rocky's eyes closed slowly as I entered him. He rested his hands on my chest and slowly grinded until he exploded on my stomach.

The next morning, Rocky made breakfast, and we worked out on the military base and toured the city. One of our stops was to the Michael Kors store so that he could introduce me to the salesperson that sold him my watch. The following days we loafed at the house watching television or eating. On some nights we went out to dinner, and other nights I prepared dinner in their kitchen. But through my eyes Rocky was no closer to a decision and doing *nothing* was a decision in and of itself.

Before I left Tallahassee, I wanted to hear Rocky's expectations, but he made every attempt to avoid the tough questions even when I cornered him in the kitchen.

"So, what are we gonna do? What do you *want* to do? " I asked.

"We had a really good time, and I don't wanna ruin it," Rocky said. "I don't wanna talk about this right now."

"I'm not trying to ruin it, but I need to know what we're doing because I'm not gonna be sneaking in town like this and waiting for you to be able to sneak out of town to see me."

Rocky was sweeping the kitchen floor and avoiding eye contact.

"Look at me," I said. "Do you want me to let go?"

"Of course not. I would never say that," he said.

"I understand that this is more difficult than you expected it to be, but if you tell me, right now, that you want me to walk with you through this and we figure it out *together,* then we can do that. Do you want us to do this together or not?" I said.

Rocky thought for a moment.

"I think this is something I have to do by myself. I don't know why, but I think this is something I have to do alone," he said.

"Ok, well, that's the answer. Let's go. I have a flight to catch," I said.

Rocky and I drove in silence to the airport. He tried to smooth things over with small talk, but I wasn't interested in saying much.

My visit to Tallahassee was the final clue that it was time for me to get off that ride. When Rocky insisted that we stay at his house as opposed to a hotel, I was well beyond my personal value system. My comfort zone was stretched past my boundaries when I stayed in the house that he shared with his wife. I wasn't ok with staying in his house, but he was ok with inviting me there to stay.

I didn't blame Rocky completely because I had culpability too, but being with a married man wasn't a part of what I signed up for. Essentially, Rocky wanted a man who was ok with sneaking, cheating, lying and living in deception with him while he was married. But I wasn't ok with living with little to no integrity, so that man wasn't me.

My mother confessed when I returned home that she knew that Rocky was married because my sister had told my aunt who then told another aunt who in turn told my mother. My mother said she empathized with Rocky because she understood how complicated divorce could be. After all, she'd been married twice, and she too had been involved with a married man for many years. But there were dramatic differences between our situations. My mother wasn't interested in JB leaving his wife to be with her, and I wasn't interested in sharing a married man.

It became clear to me that I was making an attempt to be the best *me* for Rocky because I wasn't at my best for Jacob or Carrington for that matter. In some ways, I was trying to redeem my past relationship karma through my *relationship* with Rocky.

We've all negotiated our standards at some point because we confused compromising with settling or out of loneliness, and subsequently gave more than we should have. I've known emotional masochists who latch on to relationships that are always plagued with extreme emotional lows because it feeds their emptiness. Men and women, who developed patterns of attracting hurt, and going from one painful relationship to another because they get involved with people who are consistently inconsistent or emotionally unavailable. Although I wanted to be with Rocky, I concluded that it was less important to be with him, and more important to love, and be with someone who was ready to love the way I wanted, even if it meant letting him go.

*****

I decided to have a tarot card reading with an oracle soon after I returned from Florida. I had gotten a reading by him years before when Carrington and I broke up, but I hadn't spoken to him in years. I figured it couldn't hurt to have another reading, so I looked him up and gave him a call.

"I'd like a reading about love. I know what I need to do, but I want more clarity," I said.

Right away, he asked for Rocky's full name and date of birth, as well as mine.

"Let me start by saying stability is the name of the game for you. You definitely want someone who has a stable footing—a stable energy and a stable mind. As I pull Rocky into this equation, I do get a sense of stability from him, and coupled with this is a lot of pressures on the connection. They aren't heavy, but they're evident. Talk to me about the pressures you guys are having," he suggested.

"Oh my God. I can't believe you hit the nail on the head. He's always talking to me about pressure. Ok, here's what happened. We met on May 1st and he told me on May 1st that he was married…to a woman. Their one-year anniversary was approaching the next month in June. He was working overseas at the time, but she was stationed in the states—she's in the military. So, while they were married for a year, he was gone most of that year.

"They met in the Middle East because she's military, but during the four years they dated they never really had a sexual relationship because she was a virgin. He was ok with that because he's gay and was dating guys while they were engaged. Once they were married he couldn't really perform, so they didn't have much sexual activity—" I said.

"Ok, wait, don't give me too much. I want the reading to be authentic. So, what I'm hearing is one of the reasons for the pressure is there's a marriage at the heart of this, and I haven't gotten to that yet. But I'm seeing a ten of cups in the cards, which speaks of marriage and family so it makes sense. But before that, what's crossing your connection has to deal with judgment. There's a lot of judgment on the line here. I don't know if it's self-judgment or judgment coming from family or other places, but I'm getting that there's a scrutiny here. You understand this?" he asked.

"Yes," I said.

"There's this thing about someone blowing the horn, blowing the trumpet or being put on blast. I'm getting blowing. So, is that a part of his concern?" he asked.

"Yes, it is. There was a guy that he was dealing with before we met. Once things got serious with us, Rocky cut communication with him. The guy, in turn, threatened to tell his wife everything. Come to find out, the guy had created a fake Facebook page to follow my posts. I didn't find out until I flew to Dubai, and he contacted me through Facebook. But, Rocky also felt pressure from me," I said.

"To be very honest with you, I don't see this marriage ending any time soon. And, I don't see *him* ending it any time soon. It even goes back to dealing with some of his paternal issues. I'm getting the kids' thing is a big thing for him. There's a paternal nature about him and he doesn't really recognize or realize that he can be a father in a gay relationship, but that's a big deal for him. There's also concern about his money being jeopardized," he said.

Rocky was making more than $10k a month, so he had concerns that his wife might be awarded most of the money he had saved over the course of his six years working overseas, in a divorce settlement.

"Part of your attraction to him is his financial stability because that's important for you, but the stability he brings is on a surface level. Under the surface, the emotional stability may not be there, and that's also very important for the kind of connection you want. In order for *you* to have true integrity, there has to be more emotional intelligence. There's a level of emotional intelligence *and* integrity that's *missing* here, which is also important to you. In other words, he made the decision to get married although he knew he was gay at eighteen. This is *too* unstable for you.

"Now, what I will say is the marriage will end, and it will end in a crash and burn because he needs to develop the cojones to be able to deal with this situation. Because of his lack of personal integrity it will end in a crash and burn, and it won't be pretty. Now, you on the other hand, have to decide if you want to be there to help him pick up the pieces after the fact or be there to help him deal with this as he goes through this stage of his life," he said.

"I've been pulling back. He still reaches out by phone, email or text, but I don't really hang in there as much as I did before. I just don't," I said.

"He has until June—for you. He has until June to make a bold gesture to you because your loyalties are changing. After June, you need to let him pass. Let it be. *I'm not saying wait for him 'til June.* I'm saying between now and June he has a window of opportunity *for you.* He needs to make a bold offering to you. He needs to say, 'I know I have this marriage going on, but I know what I want.' If he can do that, if he can muster up enough juice to make that kind of bold gesture, it will serve him well, and it will serve you well. But you have to decide if this is a window or if it's a door," he said

"He's told me, 'I know I wanna be with you. I'm just trying to get the courage,'" I said.

"Sure, and I get that, but you're almost like the Show Me State," he said.

"Right, you have to show me 'cause the reality is he would continue with this back and forth, sneaking around, Skyping or calling while she's in the other room, if I allowed it, and I'm not going for that," I said.

"It goes back to personal integrity, but he has to make a decision 'cause come June there will be two opportunities for real relationships for you. In fact, I see three 'cause you may have met one of them already," he said.

I withdrew from Rocky significantly with each passing day. By February, I had walked away completely. I wanted to believe something different would happen, but I knew what I knew, and knowing *when* to let go is tied to knowing when *enough* has suddenly become too little. And, if Rocky wasn't strong enough to leave his marriage, then I knew that I needed to be strong enough to let go, and walk away from the idea of us being together forever.

17 UNBREAKABLE

In the absence of Rocky in my life, I felt compelled to call Carrington to offer an apology for my part in all that went wrong in our relationship ten years before. Through my experience with Rocky, I concluded there were still some things that were unresolved for me with respect to Carrington. I thought I had left it all behind me when I saw him on the airport train that day in the Atlanta airport when I moved to L.A., but I hadn't. There was more that I needed to say to him.

I called Carrington to say what I was feeling directly as opposed to taking the coward's way out and texting him, but he didn't pick up. I left a general voice message, and he replied with a text message the following day.

"I got your message. My mom and everyone is doing well. Thanks for asking. I hope the same is true for you and yours," he texted.

"Hey, I just thought you up…you couldn't call back?" I replied.

"Not a phone person," he replied.

"Ok…But I want you to know that I came to a few realizations. What happened between us wasn't your fault, and I want to apologize for anything I did to mishandle you or your feelings. I didn't really know (at the time) how to express my feelings and didn't know how to accept the things you did to help move my dream forward. I feel responsible for not being the best me I could be for you back then. You're a beautiful person and you should always know that. I really hope you're happy. You changed my life in a good way," I wrote.

"All is well. Always has been," he replied.

*****

It was almost Christmas again, and more than eight months had passed since I last spoke with Rocky. He still crossed my mind occasionally, but not nearly as much as before. But I knew, though, that whenever he was heavy on my mind that I was also on his because that was the way it had always been with us. I still wondered how different things would've been if we were together because honestly, I hadn't met anyone that I was excited about after Rocky.

A few days before Christmas I noticed a missed call from Rocky on my cell phone, and there was a voice message.

"Hello Craig, it's Rocky. I'm just calling to see how things are going with you, and I wanted to wish you and your family a Merry Christmas. Tell everyone I said hello. I didn't expect you to answer, but I hope all is well. Ok, take care," he said.

After I listened to the message I deleted it, and made the decision not to call him back. When I got home I told my mom that Rocky had called because periodically, she would ask if I had spoken to him, and my answer was always no. Actually, for the first six months after we separated, I had blocked his number so that he couldn't reach me.

"What he say in the message?" she asked smiling.

"Nothing. Just to tell everyone hello," I said.

"Did you call him back?"

"No, for what?" I asked.

"Well, you could've called him back. You so stubborn," she said.

"It has nothing to do with being stubborn. It's the principle. If he's not ready to live his life as a gay man, then there's no need for us to talk. He knows I'm alive, so he knows I'm ok,' I said.

"You're a trip," she said. "Give me his number. I'll call him."

My mom had only met a few of the men I dated, but Rocky was one she really liked and was pulling for, so she called him and wished him happy holidays.

Two months later, I woke up from a dream about Rocky. I dreamed that he was trying to reach me, so I texted him.

"Woke up from a dream about you. Hope you're well..." I texted.

"I'm alive. Thanks," he replied.

"That doesn't sound promising," I texted.

"No...I'm studying right now," he replied.

Rocky had talked about going back to college to finish his degree, and apparently he kept his word about that.

"Ok, take care," I texted.

"You too," he replied.

A few hours later I called Rocky to talk because I missed him, but our call was very brief.

The next day, Rocky sent me a text message.

*"So, check this out. Your call caught me off guard. What I really wanted to do was be mean and curse you out, but I couldn't since my wife was right here…I missed you and all I wanted to know was that you were ok, and you blew me off when I called you back in December. Then you come contacting me out of the blue like everything was ok. *thinking* he makes me sick, uggh,"* he texted.

"LOL, I missed you too. I wanted to still be mad and that damn dream happened and I couldn't ignore it. I was angry and still bothered by what happened. I'm still bothered at times, but I can't hold on to it. I second-guessed the entire experience. I wondered if I was delusional to think things wouldn't end the way they did. I felt like you blew me off and just walked away from it like it never really mattered—like it wasn't significant," I texted.

"You took everything the wrong way, and I wasn't moving fast enough for you," he replied.

"That's not true Rocky. I wasn't rushing you. When I came to Florida, I said to you, standing in your kitchen, if you say to me, 'Craig, this is more difficult than I thought it would be, but I want

you to walk with me through this,' I would have, but, you said, 'I think I need to do this alone,'" I replied.

"You verbally attacked me," he replied.

"I felt stupid. I do apologize for speaking to you that way. That's not who I am," I texted.

"That's exactly who you are. That doesn't come out of nowhere, LOL," he replied.

"That's not who I am. That came after holding in things, and not saying them along the way," I replied.

Rocky went on to say that I hurt him with my words. But my words didn't hurt him nearly as much as his *choice* to not make a *decision,* when it really counted, had hurt me.

Slowly, Rocky and I began a texting dance once again, but this time around I expected nothing. I was removed from the feelings I had before. Frankly, I pitied him and lost quite a bit of respect for him for staying, but resolved ultimately that he had to leave his marriage only when he was ready, not for me or anyone else.

Rocky still didn't quite know who he was, yet. Not as a gay man, but as a person. He was still living for public perception. Rocky had mastered the art of deceiving, not just his wife, but also his family, the world, and most importantly himself.

I believe that we crossed paths at a time when he wasn't as ready to end his marriage as he thought he was. Perhaps, in the greater context, my role in his life was to model courage, and hopefully give him the push he'd need when he was finally ready.

A month later after Rocky and I had reconnected, he called to tell me that his wife found the greeting card I sent him in the care package when he was still working in the Middle East.

"Hey. What are you doing?" he said.

"Nothing, just waking up really," I said.

"She found the card you sent me, and she went on my Facebook page and found your Facebook page," he mumbled.

I could hear Rocky's voice trembling.

"What card? Oh! I didn't know you still had it. How did she find it? Where was it?" I quizzed.

"It was in my home office. It wasn't out, but it wasn't put up either," he said.

"Where are you?" I asked.

"I'm at school trying to get ready for an exam today. My head is fucked up right now," he said.

"So, what, she called you?" I asked.

"No, she took a picture of the card and texted it to me, and screenshot your Facebook page," he said.

"Oh God...What did the card say? I can't even remember," I said.

"You said something about me coming home and you wrote, *I love you,* inside," he said.

"So, what did you say? Did you lie?" I asked.

"Well, yeah," he admitted.

"What did you say?" I pressed.

"I just said you were a guy that liked me," he confessed.

"She can't possibly believe that… But why lie? This was your opportunity to come clean! I mean, this isn't how I wanted to see it happen, but don't lie because it feels easier," I said.

Rocky sniffled on the phone.

"I can hear you crying," I said. "It's gonna be ok. Sometimes the hardest thing and the right thing are the same."

"I need to go. Let me call you back," he said.

"Ok," I said.

Part of me believed that on a subconscious level Rocky left the card out to be found because he wanted her to find it. Otherwise, he would have hidden it, or destroyed it before he went home permanently.

Every few days I checked on Rocky to see how he was holding up because I loved him. He admitted that things were extremely tense at home. Rocky said that his wife lunged at him out of anger, and that she moved into the guest room for several days, but eventually moved back into their bedroom.

Another month passed and I received an email from Rocky's wife on Facebook.

Mr. Stewart,

You don't know me; however, you do know my husband, Rocky. I am writing you so that I can have closure. I recently found a card addressed from you to him dated back in 2013. I would like to know if this is old news or if whatever it was you shared is still going on. I've determined that my husband has attempted to work in deception and has failed miserably. I don't trust much that comes out of his mouth these days. Let me know the truth.

Leslie

I called Rocky to tell him about the email his wife sent me so that he was aware, but I never replied back to his wife because that matter had nothing to do with me—it was none of my business. She had all the proof she needed if she was ready to be honest with herself.

I resolved that there's a crop of women who are well aware that the men they love *love* other men, and it was obvious that Rocky's wife was ok being one of those women. Perhaps, she was more concerned with him being *faithful* in the marriage, and less concerned with him being gay.

EPILOGUE

We teach ourselves many things while hiding in the closet—how to cheat, how to sneak, how to pass as straight, and how to lie, but not just to ourselves—to those who know and love us. With that, we program ourselves and are *conditioned* to believe it's wrong to be gay.

Once we come out of the proverbial closet we forget to *re-teach* ourselves the things we learned while locked away in the closet. Thus, many of us bring unhealthy thoughts and behaviors with us into the gay community. Sneaking and cheating for the sake of hiding and lying about our sexuality as teenagers teaches many of us how to be dishonest liars as grown men, and many *never* outgrow the behavior even after they accept their sexuality.

I have more understanding now about why some gay men marry women. Some of these men marry women to prove their masculinity to themselves, while others jump the broom for a chance at happily ever after because it is their belief that they'll never find the consistency or longevity they desire with a man—they fear being alone for the rest of their lives. It's believed by many that gay men are incapable of offering longevity. Thus, these men marry women with the hopes of finding the companionship they crave with another man.

Next there are men who *remain* in marriages while maintaining gay extramarital affairs because they believe it's easier to juggle marriage with deception than to be gay *fulltime* in the light. Before, I thought this lifestyle choice—gay men marrying women— was only cowardice and pure deception, and on some level I still do. However, I understand that there's a subculture of married men who forgo their happiness and freedom to live their truth by remaining in their marriage because they helped build that life—a family—and leaving would feel like abandonment. In essence, these men *choose* to selflessly suppress their needs in the way a parent puts off his or her dreams to provide for their children as opposed to running after their dream. So, to them, it isn't deception at all. Rather, it's fulfilling a commitment they've made.

It could be deemed selfish of a married gay man to walk away from a life he helped to build, or it could be deceptive if he stayed, depending on who was judging the man living on the periphery of both worlds. Whichever the case, I'm grateful for the courage to live my truth everyday unabashed and without apology.

A great number of gay men are emotionally vacant and emotionally inconsistent because many of us lack the emotional language to communicate how we feel, and what we need as *gay* men. To that end, we're *in part* a community of men with wounded hearts and tortured souls attempting to love each other *without* doing the proper self-healing first.

The truth is, before we ever speak our truth to anyone we admit to ourselves that we're gay, and I believe there's an emotional trauma that occurs before or during the coming out process that affects self-esteem. Oftentimes, we harbor insecurities around coming out, and those insecurities latch onto self-esteem, depleting it.

Whether we incur emotional wounds while hiding in the closet or simply by default in telling people our truth, very few gay men come out of the closet unscathed. Those emotional scars lead to the emotional blocks in our relationships that prevent us from building emotional communication with one another, which results in us giving up on our relationships without explanation. And if we stay in them, we spend a considerable portion of the relationship trying to heal our partner.

I've never enjoyed the inconsistencies that come with dating, and I've almost talked myself out of great things because I was overanalyzing and over thinking whether or not we were on the same page instead of being in the moment. But, I've also had experiences that left me disappointed because I thought there was mutual interest. Yet, things quickly burned away without a good explanation. I began wondering if I was the problem—if I was *undateable*—or, if this problem was consistent with dating in the gay community.

The first heartbreak I ever experienced was admitting to myself that I was gay—it was painful to face that truth. Many years passed before I acted on the feelings. Even after I came out to family and friends I still quietly grieved my truth, while carrying my broken, bleeding heart with me into every friendship and relationship that I had along the way. That bleeding heart poisoned every chance I had for healthy relationships. I secretly sabotaged my chances at healthy relationships, because on some level, I thought it was impossible for two men to have a healthy relationship free of deception, cheating and other dysfunctions.

The first guy that I *dated* negatively shaped my expectations. Dating Farrell, whom I wrote about in part one of my memoir, *Words Never Spoken*, led me to believe that all of the men that I would date after him would also be conniving and untrustworthy. Sometimes we create a story in our mind and because that's the story we *choose* to believe, we continue to draw that energy to us. Thus, our past experiences corrupt future opportunities. And, in most cases we develop an unhealthy dating pattern instead of recalibrating so that we choose better partners for ourselves.

I was also having trouble reconciling the things I was taught in the Black church by the Black family and the Black community about being gay with what was indigenous to me. The same will be true for you until you stop your bleeding heart, suture it, and allow it to heal.

A surplus of gay men come into the gay community broken—looking for someone to put our broken pieces back together, while having sex for validation or recreation because it seems like fun at first. I believe our brokenness stems from years of carrying shame about being gay, and in some cases being called "sissy," "fag" or "punk" by strangers, and sometimes even by family.

Most Black men, gay and straight, are raised by women in single parent households with no demonstration of a long-term partnership, so it's no coincidence that there are so few examples of solid Black gay relationships that are visible in our community. Additionally, there are very few examples of Black gay men in loving relationships being modeled in media.

We live in a world where people share more than too much on social media. It's important to keep some things sacred—intimate conversations about sex included. Ultimately, *some conversations should be reserved for your relationship, and those things should never be discussed outside of it with anyone—good or bad*—and certainly not as a Facebook status update, a Tweet or a post on Instagram.

A common mistake many of us make while dating, and in our relationships, is telling too much of what's going on behind the scenes of the relationship to friends or family. I had a terrible habit of sharing with friends all that wasn't going well with whomever I was dating without *balancing the story* with all that was great about it too. Out of frustration I only told what was bothering me *at that moment*. I was quick to complain about what I was *unhappy* with, but seldom offered reports of all that was special—the things that lured me to the relationship in the first place.

Naturally, my friends' perceptions were slanted, and their attitude towards my mate was skewed, which resulted in them disliking my companion and offering advice that wasn't always the best for the relationship. This was partially my fault, because I hadn't given them a full picture from which they could properly advise me.

I'm asked all the time if I believe two men can have a healthy, loving, long-term, monogamous relationship, and the answer is yes. I believe that what you desire you can have because whatever you're looking for is also looking for you. Our fears sometimes cloud hope—convincing us that what's possible is *impossible*. But, *fear can only paralyze us if we allow* ourselves to hear doubt *louder* than hope.

Sexuality is instinctive—it's how we're wired. It's not decided. Being gay is more than sex—it's a responsibility. Know that every time we hide our relationships we offer an apology for who we are. And every time you lie about *who you are*, by hiding your truth, *you diminish a bit*.

We're God's most gifted and talented people. Stop looking for evidence that supports your insecurities. Get free. Live your truth. Life is about choices, so live with intention.

THE END

www.CraigTheWriterStewart.com

www.ingramcontent.com/pod-product-compliance
Lightning Source LLC
Chambersburg PA
CBHW031950080426

42735CB00007B/340